COMPUTER USE
IN HUMAN SERVICES

COMPUTER USE IN HUMAN SERVICES

A Guide to Information Management

Dick Schoech, Ph.D.

*University of Texas,
Arlington Schools of Business,
Social Work and Urban Studies*

HUMAN SCIENCES PRESS

72 Fifth Avenue   3 Henrietta Street
NEW YORK, NY 10011 ● LONDON, WC2E 8LU

Copyright © 1982 by Human Sciences Press, Inc.
72 Fifth Avenue, New York, New York 10011

Printed in the United States of America
123456789 987654321

Library of Congress Cataloging in Publication Data

Schoech, Dick.
   Computer use in human services.

   Includes bibliographical references and index.
   1. Social service—Data processing.   2. Social
service—Information services. I. Title.
HV41.S33   361'.0028'54   81-6407
ISBN 0-87705-502-5   AACR2

To my parents

Contents

ACKNOWLEDGEMENTS

This book evolved over the last $3\frac{1}{2}$ years from an exploratory "state of the art" survey, to a doctoral dissertation on the use of computers in human services, and finally into the present book on computerized information management in the human services. The process was one of a student and practitioner in the human services discovering the rapidly moving fields of computers and information management. The search was interdisciplinary, drawing on academicians, practitioners, and the literature in human services, management, systems analysis, and urban studies.

Many people contributed to this book along the way and their contributions are appreciated. I wish to especially thank Tony Arangio, Chairman of the Planning and Administration Sequence, School of Social Work, University of Texas at Arlington (UTA), who sponsored the UTA Organized Research grant for the initial survey; and Larry Schkade, Professor of Systems Analysis and Urban Studies (UTA), who with his vast experience and divergent and questioning mind, helped me explore the information revolution and its ramifications for the human services.

Special thanks are also deserved by those who reviewed and commented on this document somewhere along the way: Wayne Duehn, Chairman of the Direct Practice Sequence, School of Social Work, UTA; Temple Baker, Research Associate, UTA; Bill Ayers, Professor, School of Social Work, University of Tennessee, Knoxville; Larry Secrest of Standard Meats, Ft. Worth, Texas; Dick Shute, Director, Office of Program Systems Development, Office of Human Development, Department of Health and Human Services; Cecil R. Wurster, Chief, and Walter A. Leginski, Social Science Analyst, Statistical Program Development Branch, Division of Biometry and Epidemiology, National Institute of Mental Health, Department of Health and Human Services; and John Paton, President of CMHC Systems, Inc., Worthington, Ohio.

Those who write know the importance of secretarial help. I am indebted to Dorothy Pauley, Donna Turner, and Cindy Viol of the UTA School of Social Work.

Finally, my wife Sharon deserves mention for her support throughout the project and for being very understanding at times when I took this research and writing too seriously.

INTRODUCTION

The world is in the midst of an information revolution that is being powered by the computer and spurred on by the miniaturization of electronics. This information revolution involves the need for and the collection, management, and use of data throughout our society. The paradox of the information revolution is that we are suffering from information overload, too much information vying for our attention, while at the same time never getting all the information we need. We in the human services are especially plagued by the need for massive amounts of data and information, but have not yet come to grips with the best methods to manage that information to improve our service delivery systems.

This book is an analysis of our attempts to use the potentials of the information revolution for better management of the information we have available. It addresses the underlying process of decision making, since the process of providing human services is a combination of thousands of decisions made by executives, managers, therapists, caseworkers, paraprofessionals, and secretaries in the human service delivery system. Decision making can be improved in three fundamental ways. The first is to change the decision makers by expanding their theoretical comprehension, analytical abilities, experiences, and skills. This occurs daily in universities, conferences, and workshops throughout the world. The second way to improve decision making is to improve the environment in which a decision is made, the "task environment," as the 1978 Nobel prize winner, Herbert Simon, calls it. This can be done by changing the structure and climate of an organization or group—that is, making the situation conducive to making a better decision. Organization dynamics, job enrichment, and office and building design are just a few of the activities with this aim. The third way is to improve decision making, and the focus of this book is to improve the information on which decisions are based. The overall goal of this book is to help human service practitioners manage data and information in such a way as to improve their decision-making ability.

Managing the information on which decisions are based is by far the simplest approach to improving decision making. To change people and the task environment has proven extremely difficult and as an inexact science is fraught with unintended side effects. Managing information is relatively easy; the biggest problem, however, is not managing information but the impact this information change has on people and on organizations.

The information a decision maker uses has traditionally not been seen as an entity in and of itself capable of being managed as are other organizational resources. With computers, however, data and information can be collected, stored, manipulated, and retrieved easily and rapidly and at a very low cost. This is why this book is appropriately entitled *Computer Use in Human Services: A Guide to Information Management*. Computers are the tools behind all the data management applications discussed. Although conceptually the computer is a machine totally separate from data management, it is a practical fact of life that most modern information management applications could not exist without.

It is the computer that makes the management of data and information an emerging field of study. The computer is the core technology and also the mechanism for linking together other information technologies such as television, video tapes and disks, lasers, and word processing and telecommunications. The result is the field of study called "information management." The goal of the field of information management is to develop a collection of tools, techniques, concepts, and principles that will allow an organization to structure the information it generates so this information furthers decision making that results in goal achievement. This book is designed to help the human service agency use the computer to organize its information in such a way as to improve services to its clients.

Futurists predict that today's largest computers will be reduced to a $200 pocket-size calculator style device by 1985, and that by the end of this century the entire Library of Congress could be self-contained in a small personal microcomputer (Roland, 1979, p. 83). The impact of this information capacity on our decision making will be tremendous, but only if the information is well organized, well managed, and used.

The purpose of this book is to set directions for managing information to improve decision making in the human services. Part I defines the field of information management and provides the technological and organizational environment in which information management occurs. It provides the "big picture" or the context from which to view the chapters that follow.

Part II presents the theoretical underpinnings of information management. Each theoretical perspective gives us another view that aids in our ability to analyze and generalize about information management. As with the story of the blind men describing the elephant, each views a different part and each accurately describes what it finds. We need many descriptions, however, if we are to arrive at an accurate picture of the elephantine field of information management.

Part III looks at information management in three different types of organizations, business, government, and human service. Although each type of organization operates with a unique set of contingencies and problems, much can be learned by analyzing experiences across organizational types. This is especially true for human service organizations that are 5 to 10 years behind business and local government in information management.

Part IV is a distillation of guidelines, limitations, and problems developed from the theoretical perspectives of Part II and the experiences of Part III. It is a list of generalized "do's" and "don'ts." These are not ironclad, but are intended to open up thinking and analysis and to stimulate one to address as many of the potential alternatives and problems as possible before implementing any information management application.

Part V looks at the future and then presents a series of recommendations on how human service professionals can prepare themselves to work in and control this future. It is basically optimistic and protechnology. The book ends with a chapter on the negative potentials of computerized information. This last chapter tries to make us step back and think about what deleterious effects our fascination with information technology can have on our lives if we simply acquiesce to changes rather than control them.

This book is intended for human service professionals, especially those whose major task involves decision making using large quantities of data and information. For the day care worker or the art therapist, this book may be no more than a curiosity; but for administrators, caseworkers, and therapists, this book discusses concepts they must use and presents issues and problems they must face in the years to come. It is not intended to be a highly specialized or technical guide. Several technical guides are already available and are referenced. Rather, it is a book that can be useful before one is ready to use a specialized technical guide. It helps one develop a framework from which to approach information management, ask the appropriate questions, and consider the relevant alternatives. Thus one of the major uses of this book is in the education and training of human service personnel on information management.

Those wanting a book on human service management information systems should find this book useful, for the management information system literature often presents a very narrow perspective. This book discusses management information systems throughout, but only as a major application in the field of information management.

It is hoped that this book will show human service agencies the necessary steps that must, and inevitably will, be taken to make some sense out of the massive amounts of data and information they now collect. By improving an organization's data and information management efforts, decision making throughout all its levels will be improved. The end result, and the overall goal of this book, is the improvement of services to clients, since meeting their needs is the only reason for the existence of human service professionals.

INFORMATION MANAGEMENT AND ITS CONTEXT

Viewing information as an entity in and of itself implies that information has a history and a future and that information can be managed to meet our needs. Part I tells us where we have been, where we are going, and what information management is about. It presents the overall context within which the rest of the book should be read.

Chapter 1

THE CONTEXT

The Information Revolution

For approximately the last hundred years we have been in the early stages of an information revolution that shows every sign of being as fundamental as the industrial revolution. It could be called the "third information revolution." The first was the revolution that occurred due to the invention of symbols that allowed information to be written down. The second was the printing press, which involved the mass production of written information and circulation of information not only to the rich, but to all levels of society. The third revolution comprises the automation of information that allows for instant communication across the world, massive and rapid storage and retrieval, and the development of new communication forms (Simon, 1977, p. 1186).

The information revolution can also be seen as a second industrial revolution. The first industrial revolution, or mechanization, involved the freeing of men's hands by machines. The result is that physical labor is constantly being replaced by machines, especially in the more repetitive and routine physical tasks and those involving a large-scale human effort. The second industrial revolution, or the information revolution, is the freeing of men's minds by machine, especially in the more repetitive routine mental tasks and those involving massive analyses of data. The information revolution seems destined to change our lives as dramatically as the industrial revolution.

We can view our world in terms of preindustrial, industrial, and postindustrial countries. In preindustrial countries the primary work involves the extraction of natural resources as in agriculture, mining, fishing, and timber. The strategic resource in preindustrial societies is a country's natural resources. In industrial countries the primary work involves the application of machine technology to the fabrication of goods—for example, steel, cars, television. The strategic resources are capital and labor. In the postindustrial societies the primary work involves the provision of human services—for example, health, education, and welfare—and the provision of professional services, such as computing, research, and planning. The strategic resources in a postindustrial society are knowledge and information.

Only in a postindustrial society such as the United States are innovation, change, and growth derived from the codification of theoretical knowledge. In an industrial society, innovation, change, and growth are derived from mechanical inventions, whereas in a preindustrial society they are derived from the discovery of new resources (Bell, 1979, pp. 22-23). The point to be made is that a society's dependence on knowledge and information increases dramatically as it changes from a preindustrial to an industrial and, finally, to a postindustrial society. The United States and other postindustrial countries are fast becoming information-based economies. A recent nine-volume study by the U.S. Department of Commerce concluded that "46% of the Gross National Product is derived from producing, processing, and distributing information, with almost half the country's labor force involved in 'information activity'" (Gregory, 1978, p. 9).

The computer is the central technology behind the information revolution. The computer's role in the information revolution can be compared to electricity's role in mechanization. The computer is the central driving force without which the revolution could not occur. Other technologies and their applications such as television, lasers, communication satellites, electronic mail, robotics, and artificial intelligence are also involved, but the essence of the information revolution is the binding of all these technologies to the computer. Once linked to the computer, and thus to each other, these technologies take on far-reaching capabilities which we are just beginning to discover.

Spurring on the information revolution is the miniturization of electronics. Microelectronics, a by-product of the space age, allows for tremendous information-processing capacity by very small units and, most importantly, at a very small cost.

The most dazzling aspect of the information revolution is the speed at which it is occurring. Figure 1-1 points out

Figure 1-1.   Overall Growth of Computerized Data Processing in Business

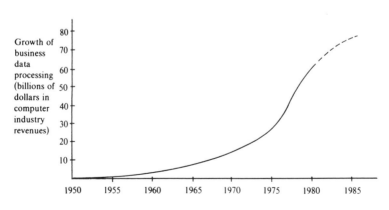

Note. Adapted from Getz (1978), Getting (1977), and Kirkley (1979). From "What Human Services Can Learn From Business About Computerization" by D. J. Schoech & L. L. Schkade, *Public Welfare*, 1980, 38 (3), 20. Reprinted by permission.

that we are still in the middle of the rapid growth curve of computers and communications. Yet, we as a society have not begun to harness our present communication technology to meet our needs. Technology is running away from our ability to use it, control it, and integrate it into our society. From all indications, technology will continue its rapid developmental pace while society reacts with what Alvin Toffler (1970, p. 2) labels "future shock," or the shattering stress and disorientation induced by too much change in a short period of time.

One of the more sobering aspects of the information revolution is that it is occurring rapidly on a worldwide scale. To escape industrialized society, man moved on and discovered new lands. Today there are no new lands. Few countries exist that are not touched by information technology such as the radio or television. Some authors look to outer space as the last real frontier or escape, but space exploration is itself built on computers and other technologies based in the information revolution. We must begin to face the fact that the information revolution is not just changing our society, it is becoming the major change in the world today. The direction seems set; there is no turning back. Our Western, high technology, information-dominated society and the world view on which it is based seem to be the direction in which all countries are being pulled, not with any planning or foresight, but simply because technology increases power and control in today's world.

This book examines one impact of the information revolution: the effect it is having on the management of the organizations in our society. Although it draws from the theories, literature, and experiences of business and government, the book's primary focus is on human-service organizations or those that are formed by government and private funds to provide services rather than produce a tangible, marketable product.

The managing of information as an organizational entity is rapidly evolving. The best way to view this evolution and its impact on human service organizations is to examine trends in computer technology, trends in the organizational use of computerized information, and trends in the human services.

Trends in Computer Technology

The best way to trace the trends in information management is from the perspective of the major structural components of an information management system. They are (a) computer hardware, that is, the central processor and the internal or core memory; (b) computer software, that is instructions written in computer languages that tell the hardware what to do; and (c) peripherals or any device connected to, yet distinct from, the hardware such as an input device, for example, a keyboard or computer card reader; an output device, for example, a TV screen or printer; and external storage devices, for example, external tapes or disks.

Computer Hardware or Central Processing Components

Computer hardware is at the leading edge of the information revolution. Its rate of achievement is faster than most people can comprehend.

> Those outside the electronic priesthood often have trouble grasping the principles of the new microtechnology or comprehending the accomplishments of the miniscule computers. The usual human sense of scale, the proportion between size and capability, the time ratio assumed between thought and action are swept into a new and surreal terrain. (The Computer Society, 1978, p. 44)

Computer hardware is becoming more sophisticated due to recent advances in the semiconductor field. "The cost of circuitry used in data processing equipment has tumbled one-hundredfold since the development of the integrated circuit" (Spangle, 1978, p. 16). We are now entering the fourth generation of computers since their birth in the early 1950s. Progress has been phenomenal: "A single large-scale integrated circuit in 1977 can contain more active elements than the most complex electronic equipment ever built 25 years ago" (Noyce, 1977, p. 1102). To give an example of the progress being made, Intel Corporation recently introduced a microcomputer on a .41 x .54 cm chip which includes a 16,000-bit read-only memory, a 512-bit random-access memory, and a central processing unit that can perform 100,000 arithmetic and logic operations per second. (A bit is one binary digit of information, either a 1 or a 0 in computer language.) The cost of the chip in quantity is under $10 (Kahne, Lefkowitz, & Rose, 1979, p. 79).

The 25-year span of computer development is a very short period of time. If we look over the next 25 years, we see that technology is leading to a very small, low-cost, dedicated, stand-alone computer which has been described as follows:

> A pocket-sized, hand-held device that unfolds to reveal an alphanumeric keyboard, flat color screen, speaker, microphone, video camera, and receptacles for plugging in small mass-storage modules. It will have one or more jacks for plugging into the communications network and perhaps an antenna for communication through local relay stations or satellites. Some ... may be small enough to be worn like wristwatches. (Roland, 1979, pp. 84-85)

Companies are scrambling to develop and mass produce this basic computer, which is expected to have public acceptance and sales similar to that of other recent microprocessor devices such as the calculator and the digital watch. The predicted technological development timetable looks as follows:

1972—Calculator-on-a-chip

1976/77—Computer-on-a-chip

1978/80—Computer-on-a-wafer

1980/83—Microcomputer-on-a-wafer

1982/87—Maxicomputer-on-a-wafer (Joseph, 1978, p. 76)

It is clear that the major problems in the future will not be technological and economic but will result from the ever-broadening range of applications. Some of the predictions about the applications of computer technology follow.

1. Progress or change in the advanced, imaginative use of computers will be despairingly slow—certainly much slower than in the first 25 years of computer development.
2. Man will continue to increase the number of "intelligent" tasks for computers faster than he does for himself.
3. Major efforts will be directed toward the use of computers for increasing public accountability.
4. In spite of all man-made constraints, there will be an irreversible but slow trek to realize with computers, forms of intelligent behavior that are essentially limitless, transcending man and computer taken separately (Davis, 1977, p. 1102).

A summary of the past and future 25 years of computers reveals the rapid pace with which computers are becoming an integral part of our daily lives.

1. Pre-1950 era: The pioneering era when basic concepts were developed by a few people.
2. The 1950s: Considered the era of experimentation and development.
3. The 1960s: The era of consolidation in which computers become an integral and inherent part of business, industrial, and military organizations.
4. The 1970s: The era of exploitation, in which computer and data processing equipment have become a sound business.
5. The 1980s: The era of maturity in which industry and technology begin to stabilize, despite continuing rapid growth.
6. The post-1990s: The pervasive era for computers. Every aspect of our daily lives will interface with computers in one way or another. A typical middle-class home will contain 20 or more computers by the early 1990s (Hobbs, 1976, pp. 9-10).

Computer Software

Software contains the directions that make the computer operate. It is the totality of programs, and documentation routines that make the hardware perform its data processing function (programs are sets of instructions for performing computer operations). Included in software are manuals, documentation, and administrative policies (Burch, Strater, & Grudnitski, 1979, p. 78).

Software can be categorized in several ways. The major distinction is between systems software and applications software. Systems software controls the operation of the computer. It performs such routine internal tasks as keeping track of where data files reside and translating application programs into codes that the central processor can understand. Applications software consists of the programs that the user needs to solve a problem or perform a task, for example, generating a report or performing a statistical analysis. Applications software can be developed by the user for specific purpose tasks, such as a special report, or bought from a computer manufacturer or software vendor for general purpose tasks, such as monthly payroll and accounting. The present trend is for applications software to be either interactive or conversational. With interactive software the computer keeps up with and responds immediately to the requests or inputs of the user, that is, the computer responds in real-time. Conversational software is interactive and, in addition, asks questions of the user and takes action based on the user's responses.

Software can also be categorized as either resident, that is, present in the system or in internal memory—or nonresident—that is, external to the system. An example of resident software is what is called an "operating system" or the interface between the user's programs and the internal operations of the computer, that is, a monitor. An example of nonresident software is that which is available on many microcomputers where the software is on an external floppy disk and must be loaded into the central processor in order to use the system. The distinction between resident and nonresident is especially important for small computer systems in which the size of the internal memory is of concern. When nonresident software is loaded into the system, it may occupy a substantial portion of the internal memory—for example 30%—and limit the manipulation capacity of the system.

Man communicates with most machines by use of levers and valves. Man communicates with a computer by the use of computer languages or the set of characters, words, rules, and procedures to which programs must adhere. The languages in which programs are written vary in the knowledge and skill required for their use. There are three levels of languages: machine languages, or strings of numeric codes that communicate directly with the computer; assembly languages, which use words that the computer translates into strings of codes—for example, Load, Total; and high-level languages, which use English-like instructions that the computer translates into machine language—for example, BASIC, COBOL, FORTRAN. High level languages are procedure-oriented; that is, the user develops the program from a standard set of constructs. The trend in computer languages is to make them easier to use by those who have little computer knowledge and skill. This trend, which usually goes under the umbrella term of "nonprocedure-oriented language," allows the user to specify needs and then the software to select, write, and perform the most appropriate program to meet those needs (McCracken, 1978, p. 26).

With hardware reaching the commodity-item stage, software is taking on increasing significance. In 1955, software accounted for 15% of a system's total cost; in 1977, it was 75%, and in 1985, it is likely to exceed 90% (Software, 1977, p. 12). There are three major sources of software: (a) manufacturers, to accompany their hardware; (b) in-house; and (c) the fastest growing source, professional software firms. The software field is growing rapidly because it is replacing the need for expensive continuing data processing services. Software is becoming increasingly conversational, efficient, and tolerant of user errors by anticipating common mistakes and either correcting for them automatically or clarifying the errors with the user. While data processing systems are becoming more complex, the number and skills of operators and programmers required to operate the systems are decreasing (Exley, 1977, p. 396).

Software is thus being developed to give the inexperienced user total access to massive computer capacity. This access will be compatible with the user's logic and language, and the conversation between man and computer will resemble conventional English such as someone dialoguing with an expert. In this case, however, the expert will be the computer with massive data manipulative capacity and with potential access, via telephone, to all automated information in the world. When this begins to occur, the information revolution will be reaching maturity.

Peripherals

Peripherals are storage or communication equipment that are distinct from, yet tied into, the central processing unit of the computer. The most important peripherals for information management are data entry devices, massive storage devices, and output devices.

Data entry devices take a variety of forms such as computer card readers, typewriters (often combined with TV-type video displays), mechanical readers of print and handwriting, and voice recognition devices. The two that seem to show the most promise for the 1980s are the keyboard and the mechanical reader. Cost-effective devices that understand all spoken voices are probably decades away. Intelligent terminals, a keyboard and video display that uses small computer chips to perform low-capacity functions, are also predicted to increase in popularity during the 1980s (Caswell, 1979, pp. 84-86). Roland (1979) predicts the cost of a keyboard in the 1980s will be approximately $5 and the cost of a video display will be $20 (p. 84).

The most critical peripheral for information management has been mass storage devices. The rapid growth occurring in computer hardware also seems to be occurring in mass storage devices. The key innovations in this area are the growth of semiconductor memories, the evolution of the bubble memory, and the vast increase in the storage capacity of traditional disk products, especially the Winchester and the floppy disk technologies. The "flubble," or a combined floppy disk and bubble memory, is also a promising development (Caswell, 1979, p. 86).

Output devices, such as low- and high-speed nonimpact printers, are also undergoing rapid development and prices will continue to fall. As Roland (1979) indicates,

A digital xerographic process is in the works that should soon make possible a high-quality high-speed printing device that prints a page at a time of computer output consisting of anything from text in any style of type to half-tone images and colors, all with an ultimate resolution as good or better than current photography can achieve. It is difficult to predict what the ultimate cost of such a device is likely to be, but it will probably be more than $500. (p. 84)

Trends in Organizational Uses of Computerized Information

Man has yet to come to grips with the technological revolution in information processing. Our terms are indicative of the situation. For example, the term "data processing" is being subsumed under "data" or "information management." We can no longer process large quantities of data unless it is managed or controlled for a specific use. Similarly, the term "management information system" is becoming inappropriate since information systems seem to be outgrowing their orientation toward only the management function. "Data base systems," "information systems," or "decision support systems" seem more appropriate terms.

Richard Nolan (1979) lists six stages of organizational experience with data processing systems ranging from the inception of the computer into the organization to the mature management of data resources. These stages are:

1. Initiation: A few, single, low-level applications such as accounting.
2. Contagion: Multiple low-level applications.
3. Control: A shift from managing the computer to managing the company's data resources and the introduction of data base concepts.
4. Integration: Increased use and movement to interactive terminals.
5. Data administration: Growth of microcomputers

and individual computers and increased emphasis on data administration as a separate function.

6. Maturity: The system mirrors the organization's data flow. (Nolan's concepts are elaborated on in Chap. 7.)

The trends running through the organizational use of computerized information are as follows:

1. Data and information developed and generated by an organization are considered a resource which, if not captured and managed, results in a costly opportunity loss for the organization.

2. Movement is from a single application to data processing modeling the information flow of an organization. The data management function thus becomes an integral part of normal daily functioning. Throughout this process, the data management function changes to mirror the organization rather than the organization changing to satisfy data management needs.

3. The management of the data system moves from lower levels to the highest level in an organization, and those in charge change from data processing personnel to management-oriented personnel. Top management location does not mean centralized control, for the control can be decentralized throughout the system regardless of where the information services executive resides.

4. The use of information management applications is moving from the operational level to the strategic level and eventually information management will permeate all levels and all decisions throughout an organization.

5. The type of information management application is changing from applications that automate a single

information collection, storage, and retrieval function, to applications that address routine choices to a limited number of measurable alternatives, to decisions in which only several of the many possible outcomes can be identified. That is, data management is moving from a limited data processing system at the operational level, to mid-level management information systems, to total organizational decision support systems. Each successive application builds on, but does not replace, the previous one.

6. Current thinking is changing from computer systems to systems of computers. The data management industry is going through its third phase in terms of characteristics of types of applications. The first was the centralization of data processing activities. The second was the proliferation of data processing throughout an organization in discrete and nonconnected systems. The third is the integration of these systems through distributed processing (Spangle, 1978, p. 15). Distributed processing refers to "any computing environment in which multiple loosely coupled computer systems implement a given application" (Kahne, Lefkowitz, & Rose, 1979, p. 78). It satisfies both central and user requirements by providing top management with central control of the total enteprise while putting advanced data processing power where the need exists and tying the whole together in a total system environment (Spangle, 1978, p. 17).

7. The medium of input changes from batch processing of computer cards, to on-line batch processing via remote terminals, to interactive conversational processing via remote video display.

Perhaps just as important as an examination of trends would be an examination of the areas in which information management has stayed the same. The main consistency throughout the last 25 years of data processing has been with the person making the decision. It seems that the person has changed only to the extent that he or she relies more heavily on data systems for making decisions. Data processing has changed to accommodate the person. For example, a conversational, nonprocedures-oriented, decision support system is not designed to change the user but to accommodate the user's personality, jargon, logic, and data needs.

The type of data needed has remained relatively constant. Basic data needs, such as budget information, have not changed as much as they have been expanded. Data management systems have allowed organizations to produce more of the needed data on a cost-effectiveness basis.

Another area that has remained relatively constant is the organization and how it functions. Nolan's six stages show the adaption of the data processing function to the organization rather than vice versa. Data processing seems to change the organization only as it goes through the six stages of adapting to the organization. In the end, Stage 6, however, data processing is a model of the organization.

Perhaps the best way to sum up the trends in organizational use of data is to quote a recent Xerox ad that read: "Not long ago, if you mentioned to someone you were in the information management field, you were greeted with a polite smile and a vacant stare. Today, you're liable to get a job offer" (*Newsweek*, 1979).

Trends in the Human Services

There are certain observable trends in the human services that have a symbiotic relationship with the need for a computerized data base. That is, the trends exist partly because of the ability to automate data, and automated data is partly responsible for producing the trends. Before the trends are listed, however, it is necessary to define human services, sometimes referred to as social services.

We will use the international perspective developed by Kahn and Kamerman (1976) from their study of the social service systems of eight Eastern and Western European countries.

> The term "social services" is internationally recognized as covering essential forms of communal provision. In the social-ist economies these are described as major forms of collective consumption. Elsewhere the rationale is that government must assure production and distribution of goods and services which should not be left to the marketplace. Despite minor differen-ces in names and some tendencies to subdivide or to combine, these five basic and familiar social services or human services are readily identifiable as education, income transfers, health, housing, employment-training. (pp. 2-3)

Kahn and Kamerman also note the emergence of a sixth social service, or what is referred to as the personal social services.

> In the most basic sense these programs strive to facilitate or enhance daily living, to enable individuals, families, and other primary groups to develop, to cope, to function, to contribute. (p. 4)

Personal social services are those addressing socialization and development; information and access; a basic level of social care and aid; substitute home or residential care; help, counseling, and advice; mutual aid and self-help; integration of programs; and controlling or supervising deviance. Some examples follow.

1. Children's services such as adoption, foster care, dependent and neglect services, and day care.
2. Aging services such as homemaker services, protec-tive services, and Meals on Wheels.
3. Family services such as community centers and counseling.
4. Self-help programs such as Parents Anonymous and Recovery, Inc. (Kahn & Kamerman, 1976, pp. 4-5).

This book focuses on the personal social services which Kahn and Kamerman view as the probable future domain of the social work profession. The focus is also oriented toward the local community and agency level rather than the state or national level. Much of the information this book presents, however, is relevant for data management in all organizations.

The major overall trend in human services is toward increased accountability and sound management. The relationship between accountability, sound management, and data management becomes obvious by examining what is meant by accountability. The demand for accountability has been categorized by the American Public Welfare Association (1977) under two headings.

> 1. "Program" accountability—that is, responsibility for the philosophy, substance, and quality of programs—requires the performance of such functions as (a) consumer participation in planning, evaluating, and revising the content of programs; (b) the provision of relevant and understandable public information; (c) measurement of the quality of services; (d) measurement of consumer satisfaction with services; (e) periodic evaluation of the results of programs within the context of other social and economic indicators; and (f) evaluation of the results obtained by focusing on target populations or on special problems or conditions.
>
> 2. "Technical" accountability—that is, responsibility for the procedures involved in management of the social services system—involves such functions as (a) the planning process . . . ; (b) the negotiation and monitoring of contracts for purchase of services; (c) the reporting of program data (e.g., which groups received which services, at what cost, in what geographic areas); and (d) the auditing of fiscal transactions. (p. 34)

Clearly the way to demonstrate accountability is through sound management techniques and these techniques require large quantities of data that are easy to manipulate and access (Hoshino & McDonald, 1975).

The following trends appear to be associated with the use of computerized data bases to insure accountability and sound management in the human services: (a) the move to quantify services, (b) the focus on program outcomes, (c) the push for service integration, and (d) recent mandated planning and evaluation. Each of these trends will be discussed in more detail below.

The Move to Quantify Services

Although business, government, and most social services do have some agreed-on output measures (number of cars produced, number of votes drawn, number of successful surgery procedures, etc.), the personal social services have had a difficult time determining acceptable units of service. A unit of service has been defined by Bowers and Bowers (1976) as "the basic ingredient to measure the amount of what has been provided to a service recipient, and in turn, what happened as a result of providing the service" (p. 5). Without this ultimate yardstick, comparisons cannot be made, relative worth evaluated, and many pressing management decisions are based on inaccurate perceptions of what is being done and accomplished. The unit of service is the essence of needs assessment, worker time and effort allocation, cost accounting, and communicaton.

Bowers and Bowers (1976) point out 13 problems in developing units of service.

1. The lack of service goals and objectives.
2. Poor service definitions.
3. No common language of service or taxonomy between programs.
4. Poor definition of service units.
5. Lack of data especially on the service delivery process.
6. No public "pricing" of services.

7. Unique nature and composition of human services.
8, Lack of project continuity in experimental efforts.
9. Linkage of unit development with worker efficiency measurement.
10. Lack of systems designers who understand the "whole" of the unit of service system.
11. Lack of supporting systems on which to build the service network.
12. Inadequate testing of a system.
13. Lack of information use by management (pp. 11-29).

Substantial progress, however, has been occurring in recent years in service quantification. A good summary of over 10 years of service quantification efforts is contained in a U.S. Department of Health, Education, and Welfare (HEW)* sponsored monograph series entitled the *Elusive Unit of Service* (Bowers & Bowers, 1976). This monograph contains examples developed by state and local human service departments, private consulting firms, and the United Way of America. A typical example appears in Figure 1-2.

Another major effort to quantify services has been occurring in HEW's Social and Rehabilitation Service using definitions contained in state human service plans developed under Title XX of the Social Security Act which was passed in 1975; HEW has attempted to classify the over 1,300 service definitions, each of which contains an average of 10 activities, into a common taxonomy of human services using a common language (Mott-McDonald, Note 11).

Not all the impetus for quantifying human services is coming from the human service profession. Inadequate regulation of human services with regard to safety, efficacy, and appropriate standards and the lack of a viable consumer

---

* In May of 1980, the DHEW was changed to the U.S. Department of Health and Human Services (HHS). The names HEW and HHS are used interchangeably in this book.

Figure 1-2. A Typical Example of a Service Quantification Effort

Service/ Output units	Unit Totals		
Chore Service	8	**Home Delivered/Congregate Meals**	33
01 One arrangement—chore services	4	26 One preparation and delivery of a meal—client's own	0
02 One hour—chore services	4	home	
		27 One preparation of a meal—central dining facility	0
Day Care—Adults	1	28 One arrangement—home delivered or congregate meals	33
03 One day—any type of day care	1		
04 One arrangement—day care services	0	**Homemaker Service**	1
		29 One hour—homemaker service	0
Day Care—Children	1,979	30 One arrangement—homemaker service	1
05 One arrangement—any type of care	7		
06 One full-time day—in-home care	737	**Home management/Functional Education**	169
07 One full-time day—care outside child's own home	1,233	31 One individual session—instructional/training	109
08 One part-time day—in-home care	0	32 One group session—instructional/training	21
09 One part-time day—care outside child's own home	3	33 One arrangement—home management and other	39
		functional educational services	
Educational Services	5		
10 One arrangement—educational training	5	**Housing Improvement**	23
		34 One arrangement—for relocation, ownership or housing	16
Employment Services	29	improvement	
11 One diagnostic assessment	22	35 One relocation—rental or ownership	1
12 One arrangement—any type of training, diagnostic	7	36 One housing improvement	6
assessment or job placement			
		Protective Services—Adults	16
Family Planning	65	37 One investigation which substantiates neglect, abuse, or	5
13 One medical contraceptive service—supply or procedure	19	exploitation	
14 One arrangement—social, educational or medical services	24	38 One investigation which does not substantiate neglect,	2
for family planning		abuse, or exploitation	
15 One individual session—education, social, information	17	39 One resolution of hazardous living situation or condition	9
16 One group session—education, social, information	5		
		Protective Services—Children	204
Foster Care—Adults	4	40 One unsubstantiated investigation	27
17 One placement—foster care home	2	41 One investigation substantiating abuse, neglect, or	27
18 One month of supervision	0	exploitation	
19 One arrangement for foster care	2	42 One resolution—court action	6
		43 One resolution—parental intervention	4
Foster Care—Children	51	44 One month of supervision	140
20 One child returned to own home or other permanent	11		
living arrangement		**Special Services—Blind**	11
21 One placement—foster care home or group care facility	8	45 One session (group or individual) training/education for	1
22 One month of supervision	32	client or caretaker	
		46 One aid/appliance	3
Health-Related Services	594	47 One arrangement—specialized services or aids for blind	7
23 One arrangement—to secure needed health services	286		
(includes admissions)		**Transportation**	350
24 One placement—medical institutions and other health	14	48 One one-way trip	322
related facilities		49 One arrangement—transportation: services	28
25 One supportive counseling session	294		

Note. From *The Elusive Unit of Service* by G. E. Bowers and M. R. Bowers, U.S. Department of Health, Education, and Welfare, Project Share Human Services Monograph Series No. 1, 1976, p. 38.

force to conteract these defects have led the courts in the last decade to become a mechanism by which appropriate and adequate treatment is being defined and mandated. According to an untitled article in the *Mental Disability Law Reporter* (Harvard Law Review, 1977), the courts have enunciated standards in three broad areas.

1.   Humane physical and psychological environments
2.   Improved quantity and quality of staff
3.   Individualized treatment plans for all residents

The standards have been surprisingly detailed and comprehensive, covering such areas as privacy, staff requirements, the use of seclusion in treatment, education and recreational programs, record-keeping procedures, patient review procedures, and procedures for evaluation and placement. Many of the decrees established extensive monitoring and enforcement requirements and mechanisms (Harvard Law Review, p. 222).

For example, in a case brought by the residents of the New Jersey Greystone Park Psychiatric Hospital, the court in over $2\frac{1}{2}$ years of litigation made recommendations in such areas as the quality and quantity of staff and the changes needed in the physical and psychological environment of the institution (Text, 1977, p. 474). In *Wuori* v. *Zitnay* (1978) the courts moved into the area of community standards. The court order required that each mentally retarded client have an individual plan of care that was periodically revised and whose implementation was the responsibility of the client's community service worker. The court went into great detail as to what constitutes an individual care plan. For example,

Each program plan shall describe the nature of the client's specific needs and capabilities, his program goals, with short-range and long-range objectives and timetables for the attainment of these objectives. The prescriptive program plan shall address each client's residential needs, medical needs, ADL skill learning needs, psychological needs, social needs, recreational needs, transportation needs, and other needs including educational, vocational, physical therapy, occupational thera-

py, and speech therapy, as appropriate. The prescriptive program plan shall include clear explanation of the daily program
needs of the client for the guidance of those responsible for
daily care. (Wuori v. Zitnay, 1978, p. 732)

Although the implementation record in mental health litigation has not been impressive, it has been a force in the effort
to quantify and document that appropriate and adequate
services have been delivered by an agency to its clients.

Focus on Program Outcomes

A second trend in human services that is encouraging the
development of computerized data bases is the focus on the
result of providing a unit of service. For example, two
management information systems, which will be discussed in
Chapter 9, incorporate outcome measures into the data base.
The Child Welfare Information System (CWIS) of New York
contains 31 indicators on which to rank agencies on child
care. Typical indicators are parental visits, discharge plans,
and movement through the service system (CWIS, Note 4).

In the area of mental health, the Community Health
Automated Record and Treatment System being implemented in several Texas mental health centers incorporates problem-oriented records along with pre- and post-client measures on a client level of functioning scale (Community, Note
3) (see Figure 1-3). (See also Smith & Sorensen, Note 21,
Chap. 8.)

The area of mental retardation is going through a
similar quantification of client outcomes. One of the more
widespread systems in use is the progress assessment chart
(PAC) system (see Fig. 1-4). The system offers a quantitative
as well as visual method of rating client progress as a result
of service intervention.

Figure 1-3(a).   Client Level of Functioning Scale (front)

Client:

_____   Case
                             No.:   _____

Date:

_____   Case   _____
                             Mgr.:

CLIENT LEVEL OF FUNCTIONING SCALE

Instructions: Circle ONE number for each area below to indicate the client's level of independent functioning in that area. Further instruction and detail available on the reverse side.

A.   Organic or Physiological Areas
      . . . Presence or Absence of major chronic or   1   2   3
            static physical or biochemical difficulties;
            major transient difficulties or well
            controlled chronic problems
      . . . Presence or Absence of significant organic
            or medical problems

B.   Emotional
      . . . Presence or Absence of situation
            inappropriate or labile emotionality
      . . . Past emotional history (e.g.: affective   1   2   3
            disorders)
      . . . Subjective feelings effecting independent
            functioning

C.   Cognitive
      . . . Current intellectual functioning
      . . . Reasoning abilities
      . . . Memory skills   1   2   3
      . . . Presence or Absence of obsessive ideations,
            delusions

D.   Perceptual
    . . . Ability to detect or discriminate
            environmental stimuli, and interpret this
            appropriately
    . . . Presence or Absence of hypochondriacal   1   2   3
            difficulties, current or historically, where
            there is no evidence of organic
            involvement

E.   Behavior
    . . . Appropriateness of current behavior to
            environmental demands
    . . . History of behavioral excess, deficit, or   1   2   3
            appropriateness

F.   Social—Interpersonal/Self
    . . . Personal hygiene
    . . . Family and marital resources
    . . . Resources from significant others   1   2   3
    . . . Social skills, ability to express self verbally
    . . . Significant capabilities in interactions with
            others
    . . . Appropriateness of view of self

G.   Work, School, and Leisure
    . . . Ability to plan time for work and leisure
    . . . History of sustained employment   1   2   3
    . . . Past educational history utilization

H.   Socioenvironmental
    . . . Stability of current living situation
    . . . Environmental resources available and being   1   2   3
            utilized
    . . . Socioeconomic status
    . . . Presence or Absence of parole or probation
            restrictions

I.   Case Management
   . . . Transportation availability to therapy
   . . . Entry into system (self-referred, court-
            referred, etc.)
   . . . Appropriateness of referral
   . . . Motivation to improve
   . . . Significant factors effecting center's service
            delivery capabilities

1   2   3

TOTAL:

Level 9 = 25-27
Level 8 = 23-24
Level 7 = 21-22
Level 6 = 19-20
Level 5 = 17-18
Level 4 = 15-16
Level 3 = 13-14
Level 2 = 11-12
Level 1 = 9-10

LEVEL OF FUNCTIONING:

Figure 1-3(b).   Client Level of Functioning Scale (back)

INSTRUCTIONS FOR CLIENT LEVEL OF FUNCTIONING SCALE

PURPOSE.   The purpose of the Level of Functioning Scale (LOF) is to access the patient's ability for independent functioning. The rater records his judgments using all available sources of information along nine dimensions. These ratings are then summed and converted to a single global LOF score reflecting the client's ability to function independently.

GENERAL INSTRUCTIONS.   Circle one number indicating the pa-tient's level of functioning in that area. A number must be circled for each of the nine areas. Sum these nine numbers and enter this sum in **total**. Look up the total on the table and find the corresponding level of functioning. Write this converted level of functioning in the LOF blank.

DEFINITIONS AND EXAMPLES for items which may be unclear.

A. Organic.   A function based on observable or detectable changes in the organs or tissues. Use whenever organic involvement is not ruled out by a physician. Ex. OBS, diabetes, epilepsy, hearing defect, paralysis, drug addiction.

B. Emotional.   Subjective feelings of the client. Problems in this area would be feelings identified as troublesome to the client or others. In most cases simple description or labeling is involved. Ex. anger, depressive mood, anxiety, fear, affection, guilt, grief.

C. Cognitive.   Activities involving the client's intellectual or cognitive processes, or processing of information. The problem is defined in terms of manifest or subjectively reported symptoms and not the underlying pathological process. This includes the client's ability to select relevant information, to remember or conceptualize information, as well as his reasoning abilities. Examples: Obsessional thinking, delusions, mental retardation, memory impairment, thought disorder, confused thought.

D. Perceptual.   Activities involving how the client perceives and interprets his internal and external environment through his senses. Problems in this area include all hallucinations, and hypochondriacal disorders, which are body sensations due to psychological factors perceived by the client as organic illness and where there is no medical evidence of organic involvement. Ex. Visual hallucinations, hypochondriacal difficulties, auditory hallucinations.

E. Behavior.   Overt behavior or patterns of behavior. Problems in this area would be behavior troublesome to the client or others. Definition is a matter of description without regard to the interpretation of the intention or meaning. Ex. Obesity, tics, suicidal behavior, run-away behavior, drug abuse, sexual dysfunction.

F. Social-Interpersonal/Self.   Reciprocal actions of two or more individuals. Also, the image or role of self which affects social interactions. Ex. Family conflict, loneliness, nonassertiveness, inadequate self-concept, self-centeredness.

G. Work, School, and Leisure.   Activities involving vocational training and placement, and school performance. This also includes avocational and recreational interests and pursuits not appropriately covered by other categories. Ex. Inability to work, unemployed, leisure outlet deficit.

H. Socioenvironmental.   Circumstances in the environment, the control of which is somewhat external to the person but affecting his independent functioning. A sample problem in this area is financial difficulties, which to some extent may be controllable by the patient, but also may be beyond his total control due to ethnic or cultural background. This would also include living condition difficulties, probation, and parole restrictions.

I. Case Management.   Factors that specifically affect only the center's ability to deliver service or the client's ability to use these services. Ex. Lack of transportation, entry into system, resistant to therapy.

Minimal or No Support.   The client is capable of independent functioning in day to day activities in the area, and requires minimal or no support or assistance to maintain his level of functioning. This may include chronic problems to which the client has adapted and is now functioning independently.

With Support.   The client is capable of functioning in day to day activities in the area only with constant or periodic external support and assistance to maintain his level of functioning and/or to prevent or forestall deterioration. External support may come from family, social service agencies, treatment, etc.

Dysfunctional.   The client is not demonstrating adequate functioning in day to day activities in the area with or without external support. Level of functioning in the area is impaired or abnormal to the extent that it severely effects his daily activities.

These definitions are global descriptions of each of the nine levels of functioning and may be used at the option of the clinician as a crosscheck for numerically derived LOF values.

Level 1: Dysfunctional in all areas, or dysfunctional in eight and marginal in one area, and is almost totally dependent upon others to provide a supportive protective environment.

Level 2: Probably not working; ordinary social unit usually cannot or will not tolerate the person; can perform minimal self-care functions but cannot assume most responsibilities or tolerate social encounters beyond restrictive settings (e.g., in group, play, or occupational therapy).

Figure 1-3(c) continued.   Client Level of Functioning Scale Definitions

Level 3: Probably not working; may be living in ordinary social unit but not without considerable strain on the person and/or on others in the household. Symptoms are such that movement in the community should be restricted or supervised.

Level 4: Probably not working, although may be capable of working in a very protective setting; able to live in ordinary social unit and contribute to the daily routine of the household; can assume responsibility for all personal self-care matters; stressful social encounters ought to be avoided or carefully supervised.

NOTE: Levels 5 through 8 describe persons who are usually functioning satisfactorily in the community, but for whom problems in one or more of the criteria areas force some degree of dependency on a form of therapeutic intervention.

Level 5: Emotional stability and stress tolerance is probably low; it is likely that successful functioning in the social and/or vocational/educational realms is impaired. The person is likely unable to hold on to either job or social unit, or both, without direct therapeutic intervention and a diminution of conflicts in either or both realms.

Level 6: The person's vocational and/or social areas or functioning are stabilized, but only because of direct therapeutic intervention. Symptom presence and severity are probably sufficient to be both noticeable and somewhat disconcerting to the client and/ or to those around the client in daily contact.

Level 7: The person is probably functioning and coping well in social and vocational (work, school, leisure) areas; however, symptom reoccurrences may be sufficiently frequent to maintain a reliance on some sort of regular therapeutic intervention.

Level 8: Functioning well in all or most areas with either little evidence of distress present, or distress present is circumscribed to one or two areas. Where little or no distress is present, a history of symptom reoccurrence suggests periodic correspondence with the center; e.g., a client may receive a medication check from a family physician who then contacts the center monthly, or the client returns for bi-monthy social activities.

Level 9: The person is functioning well in all areas, or is functioning well in most areas and is marginal in one or two areas, or is functional in all areas, and is dysfunctional in one very circumscribed area. Generally, if a client is dysfunctional in one area, it will affect other areas; so if this circumstance arises, the clinician may wish to review his assessments. No contact with the MH/MR services is recommended with Level 9 clients because they are generally able to function adequately without additional outside support.

Note. From *Community Health Automated Record and Treatment System.* Waco, Texas: Heart of Texas Region Mental Health Mental Retardation Center, 1979. Copyright 1979 by the Heart of Texas Mental Health and Mental Retardation Region. Reprinted with permission.

Service Integration

The third trend encouraging the use of computerized data base management systems is the push toward integrated service delivery systems. Service integration is an attempt to combine the numerous independent and fragmented separate social service programs into a comprehensive, rational, coordinated network of services (see the continuum in Fig. 1-5). Service integration has been defined as the linking together, by various means, of two or more service providers to allow treatment of clients in a more coordinated and comprehen-

Figure 1-4. A Sample Progress Assessment Chart of Social Development

SOCIAL ASSESSMENT

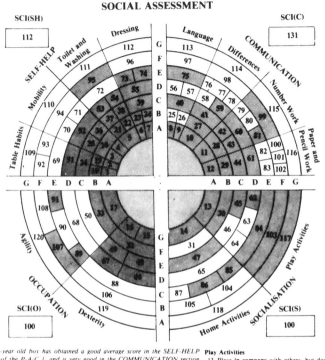

This 14-year old boy has obtained a good average score in the SELF-HELP section of the P-A-C I, and is very good in the COMMUNICATION section compared with other mentally handicapped children of his age. He is functioning well in the SOCIALISATION and OCCUPATION areas, though he should certainly be encouraged to help around the house. On the whole, this boy functions well considering his age and mental level, but the "filling-in" of some noticeable gaps would make him into a "better than average" m.h. boy.

Play Activities

13. Plays **in company** with others, but does not yet cooperate with others................ A
30. Waits "his turn," can "share" at times..... B
45. Plays co-operatively with others........... C
46. Enjoys entertaining others................ C
62. Plays competitive games, e.g., hide and seek, tag, etc........................... D
63. Acts out stories he has heard.............. D
64. Sings, dances to music, plays records....... D
84. Plays simple table games, e.g., tiddly winks, dominoes, snakes and ladders, etc........ E
103. Plays simple ball games with others, e.g., passing ball............................ F
117. Plays co-operative team games............ G

Note. From Progress Assessment Chart of Social and Personal Development, by H. C. Gunzburg. London: The National Society for Mentally Handicapped Children, 1975 (13th edition). Copyright 1973 by H. C. Gunzburg. Reprinted with permission. For further information, contact Aux Chandelles, P-A-C Dept P.O. Box 398, Bristol, Indiana 46507.

Figure 1-5. Service Integration Continuum

Nonintegrated Structure	Integrated-Coordinated or Confederated	Integrated-Comprehensive or Federated

Nonintegrated structure: Each agency has separate and autonomous responsibility for total agency administration.

Integrated-coordinated or confederated: Agencies are linked through mutual agreements or memoranda of understanding to engage in specified patterns of patient, staff, and/or information exchange, with each participant retaining its own fiscal and policy-making authority.

Integrated-comprehensive or federated: Agencies are linked by statute or charter as members of a larger system whose central authority can impose operating standards and practices upon all component subsystems.

Note. Adapted from Redburn (1977) and Schulberg & Baker (1975).

sive manner (Schulberg & Baker, 1975, p. 19). Service integration is usually seen as consisting of the following basic components (Hagebak, 1979, p. 575):

1. Common geographic service boundaries for all services.
2. Location of a number of services under one roof.
3. A sharing of core services such as intake.
4. Case planning for the client's total needs by a number of treatment specialists.
5. Assignment of the responsibility for meeting client needs to a case manager.
6. A sharing of management services such as consultation and equipment.
7. Common eligibility standards, data, or forms.

It is important to note that service integration refers to the characteristics of a service delivery system that produces goal attainment rather than to administrative procedures aimed at consolidation. Consolidation may or may not be a part of a service integration effort (Redburn, 1977, p. 265).

The federal initiative for service integration came in 1970 when Elliot Richardson, then secretary of the Department of Health, Education, and Welfare, attempted to restructure and reform virtually all HEW programs in order to gain some control over his most difficult management problem, which was the rapidly escalating demands for services and limited available funds (Lynn & Seidl, 1976, p. 111). Service integration was seen as a mechanism that would provide a central focus through which program initiatives and developmental dollars could be channeled to produce change in the system. Federal and state service integration efforts have usually been accompanied by centralized control and the replacement of social service professionals in management positions by professional managers.

Service integration has also been at the heart of many recent state social service reorganization efforts. Many states have reorganized into loosely integrated social service agencies, and a few—such as Arizona, Georgia, and Washington—have fully integrated state agencies (Heintz, 1976, p. 108). A few service integration projects are also occurring on the community level.

Without some form of service integration, information management efforts must bypass the community and proceed on an agency-by-agency basis. This agency-by-agency development could either lead to standardization and comparable data systems, or more entrenched fragmentation, with each agency developing its own system.

Three examples of community service integration will be presented to provide a better understanding of the role of data management in these efforts and to illustrate the context in which community data bases are being developed.

Portsmouth, Virginia. The nucleus of the Portsmouth system is a city-operated, central client pathway that coordinates and manages the services a client receives. Portsmouth has linked many public and private service providers to this central pathway through service contacts and formal "Memoranda of Understanding." Through the use of a management information system, the central pathway serves its member agencies by providing client data such as time in the system, dropout rate, cost-accounting data, and also by evaluating whether any changes are occurring in the community's unmet needs as a result of the system's effort (Mittenthal, 1976, pp. 147-148).

Cleveland, Ohio. Cuyahoga County (Cleveland) is attempting to implement a system similar to the British model of social service delivery by establishing a decentralized network of 26 social service teams, each responsible for the total social service needs of a geographic population base of 12,000 to 150,000. All publicly funded social services would be administered through this system and, again, contracts and service agreements would be developed with nongovernmental agencies. Obtaining exemptions from the requirements of a multitude of categorical federal programs has been one of the biggest problems so far (Yankey, Note 26; Seebohm, Note 19).

Louisville, Kentucky. Louisville's Human Services Coordination Alliance is a less integrated approach by which approximately 850 social service agencies in the Louisville area have agreed to share a common computerized intake, screening, and referral system. Little restructuring of the existing social service system was required, and it is the model of service integration most likely to become popular in the United States for this reason (DeWitt, 1977, pp. 87-91).

Information management has been one of the essential ingredients of service integration efforts because without an ability to document what is occurring in the network of community services, goal-oriented change and control are impossible. A common data base is one of the distinguishing characteristics between community agencies that are loosely coordinated entities of a network of services and agencies that are subsystems of a service delivery system.

Mandated Planning and Evaluation

Present initiatives in human service planning and evaluation are contributing to the need for greater data management efforts. These are Title XX, or the 1975 Amendments to the Social Security Act; (2) the National Health Planning and Resource Development Act of 1974 (PL 93-641, 1975); (3) Professional Standards Review Organizations (PSRO); and (4) Public Law 94-63 which mandated evaluation in community mental health centers.

Title XX of the Social Security Act mandated a statewide planning process for welfare services. State plans must meet federal criteria and address national goals. Title XX also mandated information and referral services be made available to all regardless of income.

The National Health Planning and Resource Development Act of 1974 (PL 93-641, 1975) mandated the establishment of regional health systems agencies across the United States to plan for health, mental health, alcoholism, and other federally funded human services. Coordination agreements with other federal programs as well as a substantial data collection effort was written into the law. Data management expertise was listed as one of the basic required expertise of a health systems agency, as PL 93-641 states,

> A health systems agency shall have a staff which provides the agency with expertise in the following: (i) administration, (ii) the gathering and analysis of data, (iii) health planning, and (iv) development and use of health resources. (National Health Planning, 1975, pp. 8-9)

Health systems agencies are instructed by the law to use existing data to the maximum extent practicable rather than to collect new data (p. 12).

Professional standards review organizatons, designated under Section 1152 of the Social Security Act, provide peer review of health services based on health service norms. Professional standards review organizations are basically a monitoring system and an evaluation by exception mechanism. For example, if national and local norms point to an average number of hysterectomies per 1,000 females in a certain age group and professional standards review organization data indicate that a given geographic area is substantially higher or lower than this norm, the review team would be responsible for determining whether the exception to the norm is a valid exception or a problem needing correction. Although professional standards review organizations have been plagued with problems, such as resistance, in some areas they are showing favorable results and saving more dollars than they are costing (for a discussion of peer review information systems, see Sorensen & Ertel, Note 22).

Public Law 94-63, the 1975 Amendments to the Community Mental Health Centers Act, required federally funded mental health centers to spend 2% of their operating budget on local program evaluation. This mandated evaluation has stimulated the need for systems that can collect, store, and manipulate massive amounts of program data. As computer costs continue to drop, in-house management information systems are beginning to become a cost-beneficial necessity for most centers rather than an expensive luxury. The mandated program evaluation has also helped insure that data will be used to guide service delivery (Maypole, 1978).

These trends are a few of the most important efforts toward accountability and sound management in the human services. Although each of these trends individually does not require a computerized data base, taken as a whole they show a slow movement toward the need for well-managed data bases in the human services. As computer costs rapidly decline, agencies are beginning to see the necessity for developing computerized data management systems to address their needs.

Chapter 2

INFORMATION MANAGEMENT

Introduction

To understand information management, one must understand the concepts and the language associated with the field. This chapter presents concepts crucial to any information management effort. The concepts are not based on theory, but have evolved through the last 30 years experience with computerized data processing. It is the pulling together of these concepts into a unified body of knowledge and theory that is still needed.

From a historical perspective, we can see the following major influences on organizational management thought (George, 1972).

Pre-1920s: The use of the scientific method to analyze jobs (e.g., Frederick Taylor).

1930s: The influence of sociology and the acknowledgment of the relevance of the work group to individual performance (e.g., the Hawthorne Studies).

1940s: The influence of psychology and the acknowledgement of the importance of the individual (e.g., Abraham Maslow's concepts of self-actualization and man's hierarchy of needs).

1960s: The viewing of the organization as a system (e.g., Bertalanffy's analysis of the organization as a living system).

1970s: The influence of information and computer sciences (e.g., management information systems).

These dates are only rough approximations, but each new influence helps us view management from a new perspective. This book examines the organization from the perspective of information management.

The Field of Information Management

The management of organizations is a dynamic evolutionary process. Many of the basic management concepts which we take for granted today were virtually non-existent years ago. For example, the concept of the personnel function as a separate, identifiable management function is universal today, but was nearly unrecognized in 1900 (Vyssotsky, 1979, p. 16). It is becoming clear that a similar change is occurring with the numerous separate, haphazard data and information functions, activities, and personnel which exist in most organizations today.

One example of the attempt to unite the experience and concepts of information management into a field of knowledge is the report of the Commission on Federal Paperwork (A Report, 1977) which concluded that

Information is a manageable resource. It can be planned, organized, budgeted, controlled, and evaluated using the same methods and techniques now used to manage personnel, space, real property, equipment, and supplies. Executive agencies

> should establish comprehensive information plans that incor-
> porate all the information needs and resources of the agency.
> (p. 16)

This view of information as a manageable resource, as important to the organization's functioning as its financial resources, is new to organizations. Most human service organizations can hand out their budget and give a detailed explanation of how the budget relates to each section of the organization and to the overall organization's goals and objectives. Almost none can give the same analysis and breakdown on the information needed to drive their organization. Few can tell what information management is costing their organization other than to say that a lot of time and effort is spent on reporting and paperwork. When we begin viewing information as a basic resource, it becomes obvious that information is undermanaged and quite possibly under-utilized.

The Commission on Federal Paperwork concluded that the way to control paperwork was not by the piecemeal process of paperwork simplification, mechanization, and streamlining, but by looking at why the information was collected in the first place, by whom, what role it played throughout the organization, and what contribution it was making toward goal achievement. Although the concept of managing information is not new, the concept of information as a manageable organizational resource and the idea of developing a multidisciplinary body of knowledge to address information management are major steps beyond previous efforts. The field of information management is not isolated to any one particular area, such as computer science, but cuts across many academic disciplines such as management, management science, statistics, library science, and computer science. Information management as a field of study, then, is

> An updating and integration of related information manage-
> ment principles currently dispersed and diffused among many
> different disciplines and bodies of knowledge. What IRM

[information resource management] seeks to do, then, is to bring these disparate facets together into an integrated, theoretical, and applied framework so that the organization as a whole can comprehend, install, use, and evaluate the notion without having to confront a bewildering array of different interpretations and definitions by different practicing groups. (Horton, 1977b, pp. 8-9)

This view of information management is essential, for it sets the stage for successful data processing. As Appleton (1977) points out,

In a very real sense it requires a complete psychological reorientation to computerization, not just for management, but for data processing folks as well. Even today, many companies attempt to employ the data base systems approach without making this psychological change. They feel that the employment of tools typically associated with data base concepts— data base administrators, data base management systems, data dictionaries—and modular programming will naturally lead to a data base environment. But, all too often they find that these tools, employed using conventional attitudes and strategies, do not automatically solve their data processing dilemma. (pp. 86-87)

Overall, then, the most significant changes occurring in organizations as a result of the information revolution are the coming together of the decentralized and fragmented data functions into one top-level department, and the pulling together of the disciplines, theories, and concepts related to information management into a unified body of knowledge. Some of the specific concepts associated with this movement are presented in this chapter.

Basic Definitions

Data and Information

First, the concepts of data and information need to be defined. Simply put, data are facts, and information is data that have been processed to achieve a purpose or to enhance understanding. A more formal definition follows.

> Data are language, mathematical or other symbolic surrogates which are generally agreed upon to represent people, objects, events, and concepts. Information is the result of modeling, formatting, organizing, or converting data in a way that increases the level of knowledge for its recipient. (Burch, Strater, & Grudnitski, 1979, p. 4)

This distinction between data and information is important, for to change data into information we must use the assumptions consistent with the purpose for which the data will be used. For example, the number of crimes recorded by a police department are data. The mayor may use the high number of reported crimes to show that a campaign promise to be tough on criminals has been fulfilled. The mayor has put the data into a context that changes it to information. The mayor attaches the assumption that a high number of reported crimes means a high level of crime fighting and a high quality of life for citizens. A national planner, on the other hand, may attach somewhat different assumptions to the data. The planner may see a high number of arrests as an indicator of the amount of criminal activity in the city, and thus a high number of arrests would indicate a low quality of life for citizens. As data are turned into information, and information is combined with other information in models and social indicators, we must be continually aware of the old and new purposes and assumptions the information is taking on if that information is to be validly used to improve decision making.

Throughout this book, for brevity, the terms "data" and "information" will be used interchangeably unless noted otherwise. Also, the term "information management" is used throughout this book to indicate the management of both data and information. This has been common practice in the past; for example, such terms as "data processing" and "information systems" refer to both data and information, and this book will do likewise.

Data Base

Central to the concept of information management is the concept of a data base. "A data base is a set of logically related files organized in such a way that access to the data is improved and redundancy is minimized" (Davis, 1974, p. 307). A file is a collection of similar data. The concept of a data base implies several ideas:

1. The data in a data base are naturally or logically related.
2. The data base is organized with the intention of reducing unnecessary duplication or redundancy in data—for example, the standardization of data definitions, formats, and so on; the merging of common data elements; and the replacement of information that occurs in many records by coded representations.
3. The data base is organized for quick and easy access, regardless of the physical location of the data in the data base, its order of storage, or its point of origin. This requires that multiple natural and logical paths to the data be established.
4. A data base is organized to achieve efficient and effective data management.
5. New requests of existing data do not require changes in the structure of the data base.
6. A data base is computerized.
7. The data base is a resource belonging to the entire organization, and a resource that must be managed in order that it not be wasted or misused.

The data base concept is usually contrasted to conventional files. With conventional files each application is perceived as owning the data associated with it. Little central coordination and control exists over conventional files (Lefkovits, 1977, pp. 1-2). The "ability to represent the natural data relationships with all necessary access paths is the fundamental distinction between a data base and a conventional file" (Deen, 1977, p. 5).

Data Base Management System

A data base management system (DBMS) is a grouping of computer software necessary to store, manage, and retrieve data in the data base (Davis, 1974, p. 308). Designing a data base management system is a science as well as an art, especially with large amounts of data and the need to generate multiple reports from the data.

Although the concepts of a data base and a data base management system seem rather simple, they are important; for the tendency in many organizations is to focus on the single computer application or to develop information management responsibility in each department and neglect data base development. Nolan's six stages of data processing in Chapter 1 point to the problem with this tendency. The organization, having started out with a single application in Stage 1, must continually adjust until it moves into the data base concept. Data base development is a distinct approach to information management:

> Data base development, for example, will rarely follow the same course as traditional application development. It will not start with general accounting systems because these systems are all "summary" systems. True data base development must start with the "base" data in the company. This data is always found at the lowest level of resource scheduling and costing. But here companies are most complex, most fundamentally diverse, and most inconsistent. Here, too, are vast quantities of data which

must be correlated and managed properly, and which must be combined, summarized, and extended for both financial and operational management. (Appleton, 1977, p. 90)

The Information Services Executive

To treat information as a manageable resource in an organization requires putting the responsibility and authority for information in one person, an information services executive. The term "information services executive" is preferable to "data administrator" or "management information system manager" because it points to the establishment of responsibility and authority for information management high in the organization. The information executive's position, however, is still evolving as practitioners are quick to point out.

There will be a lot of infighting before all this gets straightened out. In the end, there will arise an information services executive of power and stature similar to that of the comptroller. The rank will be that of vice-president and the information he or she controls will be viewed as one of the organization's most valuable resources. Such an executive, therefore, will sit "very close to the throne." (Gilbert, 1978, p. 151)

As the information management function moves up in the organization, the skills needed to head the information management function change from that of a data processing technician to a person who not only understands data processing but also has a thorough understanding of the workings of each department, the organization as a whole, and top-level management. The information services executive must combine the skills of communication, computing, and administration. As Getz (1978) points out, "The manager of this new area will be a generalist with a solid understanding of technology, but a better understanding of business conditions and needs" (p. 124). Because the information services executive is a generalist, he or she needs to have available specialist skills in such areas as computer hardware, computer software and programming, systems analysis and design, simulation and modeling, computer graphics and display, information security, and statistics. Some of these skills may be provided by users throughout the organization. This drawing on existing skills decreases the tendency toward functional specialization and exposes personnel to the information management function (Lyon, 1976, p. 130). Due to size, it is not cost-effective to have an information services department or even employ an information services executive in a small human service agency. The important point is that the responsibility and authority for information management be placed in the hands of a competent high-level person who has access to specialized skills when they are needed.

If information management is to have the impact desired, both the necessary skills and the top-level position must be combined. Choosing an information services executive with a narrow focus or burying the information services executive in a department such as accounting is a regressive step that will be overturned as the data function in an organization develops.

We can see that the information services executive is a natural outgrowth of the previous concepts discussed. As Minami (1976) points out, before an information services executive position can be established, certain conditions must exist:

1. Top management must be willing to take a long-range view of the cost structure.
2. DP [data processing] and line management must be prepared for the data base approach with the associated protocols, standards, etc.
3. The entire line management must view data as a resource similar to raw materials, equipment, etc. (p. 43)

Major Functions of Information Management

The major functions of the information services executive can be pulled together into five major areas:

1. Designing, establishing, and maintaining the data base management system.
2. Developing and maintaining the data dictionary.
3. Ensuring quality data and information at the lowest cost.
4. Connecting the distributed data bases throughout the organization.
5. Ensuring confidentiality and security.

These functions are not independent of each other but overlap and interact. Yet each is an integral part of the overall responsibility.

Designing, Establishing, and Maintaining the Data Base and the Data Base Management System

The core function of the information services department is to design, develop, implement, and maintain policies, procedures, and practices that collect, store, update, and retrieve all information necessary for the functioning of an organization. Some of the major tasks connected with this function follow.

Connect People with Data.   People should be connected with the data they need to make decisions. Because data are a manageable resource, the information services department is responsible for supplying the proper data to those who need it. This function is similar to the personnel department's task of supplying appropriate personnel to fill job vacancies.

Generate Reports.   Periodic and special reports must be produced.

Ensure Data Is Properly Used.   The proper use of data must be ensured and the misuse of data must be prevented in decision making. Supplying appropriate data and information does not ensure that it will be used correctly in decision making or even used at all. Training must often accompany the information to ensure its proper use. For example, in the distinction between data and information made at the beginning of this chapter, the assumptions associated with information were stressed. Although the user must assume ultimate responsibility for proper use, the information services department must provide the training and technical assistance to ensure that the assumptions and the impact of violating them are clearly understood.

Integrate Data Management into the Organization.   The data management effort must be integrated with policies and long-range plans. If information management does not become an integral part of the organization's policies—for example, new staff orientations and organizational security procedures—the system will not have its potential impact. Similarly, the information services department must play a key role in the long-range plans of the organization because the data services department's operations may be substantially affected. For example, the decision on whether to centralize or decentralize the organization structure may have direct impact on data collection reporting and use. Data flow must be geared to any new organizational initiative. Since the data base models the organization, it is possible to determine, at least from a data perspective, the impact any changes or initiatives will have on the organization.

Perform Data Audits.   Data audits must be conducted to determine whether old data should be discontinued and new data collected. Looking on data as a resource requires decisions as to what portion of all the data an organization generates is worth collecting and what is the most convenient and cheapest route by which to collect it. Similarly, there should be easily established procedures for terminating the collection of data that are no longer important.

Develop Backup Procedures. Backup procedures must be established and maintained to ensure a continuous flow of data if hardware and software fail. If data are to become a crucial resource, then their continuous flow must be assured and alternate procedures developed in case of system breakdown. For example, customers must be able to bank, purchase airline reservations, or get Social Security checks even if the hardware or software fail.

Monitor New Legislation and Laws. New legislation and laws must be monitored. Legislation such as the Privacy Act of 1974 as well as recent court initiatives are increasingly impacting data collection and dissemination. For example, in Texas a centralized child abuse registry, designed to track and monitor child abusers, was declared unconstitutional because it contained the names of reported, but nonadjudicated, child abusers. The court ruling limited the system to maintaining a list of only adjudicated abusers. The potential of the system was severely limited without the ability to receive reports on suspected abusers as they came into contact with schools, doctors, hospitals, and other social services in the community.

Evaluate the Data Management Effort. The performance of the information services department must be evaluated. Because information management is a relatively new field, the technology and methodology to evaluate its effectiveness are in the initial stages of development. Nonetheless, efforts must be made to determine whether information is improving decision making in the organization. In human service organizations, which are usually not accustomed to having data available, just the provision of data alone can often improve decision making. For example, the professional standards review organizations mentioned in Chapter 1 have resulted in medical practitioners taking a hard look at their practice because they were aware that data on their services were being collected. Documenting such changes is crucial if continued investment in data management systems is to be made.

Developing and Maintaining a Data Dictionary

A basic tool of any data base management system effort is the data dictionary or listing of the descriptions, attributes, relationships, and uses of all the data collected by the organization. The data dictionary describes and defines all the data in the data base by collecting all the relevant information associated with each data item, for example:

1. A technical description of each data item.
2. A nontechnical description of each data item.
3. Synonyms for each piece of data.
4. A physical description of each data item (e.g., length, format, range of possible values, etc.).
5. How the data item is processed, where it is stored, and how to retrieve it.
6. To what grouping and hierarchy the data item belongs.
7. Who collects the data and for what purpose.
8. How often the data are collected.
9. Who owns the data or who pays the cost of collection.
10. The uses of the data.
11. The assumptions attached to the data.

12. Quality of the data and how the quality is ascertained and verified.
13. The security and confidentiality associated with the data.

Lefkovits (1977) considers the data dictionary the cornerstone of good data management since "all too many industrial (and governmental) users have found their data base system was relatively useless until they implemented a good data dictionary system" (p. i). Lefkovits's book describes and compares six commercially available data dictionary systems for those seeking further information.

The data dictionary performs the following functions for the organization:

1. Helps control and manage the total data effort.
2. Helps coordinate and integrate the data base.
3. Helps ensure uniform use of data.
4. Helps improve communications between the information services department and the users by standardizing vocabulary.
5. Helps the user understand the meaning and limitations of data and helps ensure their proper use in decision making.
6. Helps conduct data audits by identifying all the information (collectors, users, etc.) associated with a particular piece of data.
7. Provides a constantly updated documentation of the organization's data management effort.
8. Helps in planning and designing new programs by pinpointing new data needs and showing what impact data changes will have on other programs and the total data management effort.
9. Helps the user understand the data function and thereby helps alleviate fear and resistance.

The data dictionary, then is a powerful tool because it is a written model of the organization. And, despite the rapid changes taking place in technology, data dictionaries will continue to be basic data management tools as they are developed and refined (Adams, 1978, p. 8).

Insuring Quality Data and Information at the Lowest Cost

Because data are a manageable resource, the information services department is responsible for providing the highest quality data at the lowest possible cost. The data services department must establish procedures and standards on quality and enforce them. Quality can be defined in the following terms:

1. Accuracy—for example, accuracy to the second decimal place, or 90% of the time.
2. Validity, or how well a data item represents what it is described to represent—for example, self-reported client income that is not verified may typically be overstated or understated depending on the perceived use. If the client sees income as a status symbol, overreporting may occur, whereas if income is used as a basis of determining fees on a sliding scale, underreporting may occur.
3. Reliability, or how accurate the data have proven over time.
4. Verifiability, or how often the data are verified by another source.
5. Freedom from bias, error, or the problems of reduction. Bias can be deliberate falsification and deceit, or it can be a tendency to see things from a preconceived perspective—for example, the order of a name on a ballot affects or biases the voter. Error can be caused by inaccurately measuring, collecting, recoding, transmitting, processing, or

distributing data. Reduction is the process of classifying, compressing, filtering, and inferring and may result in a loss of data quality if not controlled (Davis, 1974, pp. 42-46).

As data quality increases, data costs usually go up. The data services department must decide with the user the point where the increased quality is not worth the increased cost. Cost can be reduced by ensuring that the data are collected and verified when generated as a part of normal operating procedures. For example, if the intake worker and the caseworker automatically ask the same basic question of the client, the caseworker can be used to verify the information given to the intake worker. Data generated, but not captured, may represent an opportunity lost by an organization. For example, one company, which found that employees were using their computer-based message system rather than the telephone, used the messages that were automated as a means of obtaining information on what occurred in business phone calls. The messages were filed, retrieved, forwarded, and searched. The organization thus captured an important new set of narrative communications as a by-product of normal business procedures. Similarly, a company that maintained business calendars on the computer used the business calendar system as a way to generate a time and effort report for their employees (Gilbert, 1978, p. 145).

Another aspect to costing out information is to show information as a separate item in the organization's budget. This permits top management review of the crucial cost of managing information throughout the organization.

Linking the Distributed Data Bases of the Organization

Linking the distributed data bases is the most important and most time-consuming job of the data services executive (Bertram, 1978, p. 24). This function involves several tasks.

First, there is coordinating and integrating the contents of the distributed data bases. The concept is to tie the distributed data bases together to reduce cost and redundancy and to improve access and quality. This task is one of the biggest facing organizations today. As Spangle (1978) points out,

> Unification of languages, standardization of procedures, correlation of the contents and structure of the distributed data bases, and operation of the common message delivery network must all be carefully controlled to support the cooperating activities of the distributed environment. (p. 17)

Second, conflicts over data must either be solved or referred to the proper authorities.

Third, automatic "triggers" must be established between data bases. For example, it may be possible to determine statistically key characteristics of a Medicaid client who typically needs additional social services or who is typically associated with fraud. If these characteristics can be identified, then the intake worker providing client data into the data base, via remote terminal, can be forewarned of these possibilities and ask an additional prearranged set of questions. If the questions seem to indicate additional social services are needed or that the person has a high potential for fraud, then the system could automatically forward the client's record to the social service department or the fraud department for their attention.

Linking the distributed data bases together into a coherent integrated whole is becoming one of the most crucial tasks the information services department must face, because microcomputer technology is allowing departments and individuals to have their own computer and develop their own data bases. As Spangle notes (1978),

> The price for failure in this area is chaos! Every line manager will just proceed with purchasing his own minicomputer and follow an independent course of action. (p. 17)

Insuring Data Security and Privacy

The function of insuring data security and privacy involves matching data access with the sensitivity of the data and protecting the total system from destruction and vandalism. The first obvious step is physical security, which is similar to security procedures connected with any paper and pencil file. Protecting sensitive data must be a basic consideration from the initial design of any data management system. Design factors and access codes can be used to limit the user's ability to input data, read data, change existing data, or destroy data. Again, a costing out of data security is necessary to determine whether the confidentiality of the data is worth the cost of protecting it. Data must be protected against such activities as improper access, accidental or purposeful change or destruction, and accidental or purposeful inclusion of erroneous data. The cost of security and confidentiality seems to be one of the major considerations in moving from a centralized data base to a more distributed one (Gilbert, 1978, p. 146).

Related Concepts

There are many concepts that are important for information management. Some of these are information systems, decision support systems, and word processing.

Information Systems

Although computer-based information systems have been popular in business since the 1960s, definitional problems still exist. What constitutes an information system to the computer analyst, the human services administrator, or the communications engineer is usually substantially different. Even an 8-hour colloquium sponsored by the Society for Management Information Systems failed to reach a consensus on exactly what constitutes an information system (Hanold, 1972, p. 67).

The terms "information system" and "management information system" (MIS) seem to be used interchangeably in the literature, but usually the term "information system" refers to systems designed for decision making throughout the organization, whereas "management information system" refers to systems that are oriented toward the needs of managers. This distinction makes sense in production-oriented organizations in which the workers have little need for organized information to perform routine tasks. In human services, where worker-level tasks are many times as complex as management tasks, this distinction is less useful.

A definition of a management information system that is representative and consistent with how the term is used throughout this book follows.

> A management information system, as the term is generally understood, is an integrated, man/machine system for providing information to support the operations, management, and decision-making functions in an organization. (Davis, 1974, p. 5)

Information systems perform such functions as collecting, recording, classifying, sorting, manipulating, storing, retrieving, reproducing, and communicating.

An information system may or may not be computerized. One agency may have a highly developed manual system whereas another may have a computer-based, haphazard, and uncoordinated information gathering and retrieval effort. This distinction, although conceptually clear, is in practice harder to make, for "it has almost become an article of faith that the heart of an MIS [management information system] must be a computer" (Mason & Mitroff, 1973, p. 484). The distinction, however, is necessary lest the problems and procedures associated with developing an information system be attributed to the process of computerizing that information system and vice versa.

An information system consists of a data base, a data base management system or software that manages the data, and software and hardware oriented toward providing information to the users. An information system is the link between data processing and the users of the information. Most organizations have multiple information subsystems joined to provide information throughout the organization. Figure 2-1 presents the typical contents of a human service agency information system.

An information system must be understood in its overall context if developmental and use problems are to be avoided. Seen in this larger context,

> An information system consists of at least one PERSON of a certain PSYCHOLOGICAL TYPE who faces a PROBLEM within some ORGANIZATIONAL CONTEXT for which he needs EVIDENCE to arrive at a solution (i.e., to select some course of action) and that the evidence is made available to him through some MODE OF PRESENTATION. (Mason & Mitroff, 1973, p. 475)

Earlier information systems tend to focus on one psychological type, one class of problem, one or two methods of generating evidence, and one mode of presentation. Information systems are beginning to develop the flexibility needed to address the variety of states in each of these variables.

Information systems have advanced significantly since their use in business began in the 1960s. Early information systems were primarily housed in specialized electronic data processing (EDP) departments or subsumed under other functions such as accounting. They were used primarily for generating data and providing routine reports at the operational level, monitoring the movement of people or products through the system, developing models of systems, automating routine decison making, and providing summary and descriptive information to top management. Today, information systems have become much more flexible physically and informationally, and their focus is more on providing data and information for the decision making of middle and top-level managers.

Figure 2-1. Typical Contents of a Human Service Information System

AGENCY INFORMATION SYSTEM*

SERVICES SUBSYSTEM

File Type	Types of Data Included
Agency services	Types of programs and subprograms, geographic subareas served, admission criteria, etc.
Information & Referral	Data detailing who delivers what to whom in the community, agencies referring clients, discharges

CLIENT DATA SUBSYSTEM

File Type	Types of Data Included
Client background	Age, sex, address, presenting problem, previous treatment, medications taken, etc.
Case management	Admission date, problem type and severity, type and amount of treatment delivered, discharge and follow-up information, appointments kept, etc.

AGENCY MANAGEMENT SUBSYSTEM

File Type	Types of Data Included
Office management	Supplies, mailing lists
Personnel	Hours worked by staff member and type of activity
Fiscal management	Revenues, expenditures, billing, grants, payroll

PLANNING AND EVALUATION SUBSYSTEM

File Type	Types of Data Included
Planning	Population at risk, target population, census data
Evaluation	Efficiency, effectiveness, and productivity measures; and peer review data
Monitoring & control	Data on fulfillment of agreements, contracts, and certification and licensure requirements

* Activities common to all subsystems:
   1.   File development and modification
   2.   Printing and report generation
   3.   Searching of files, aggregations, descriptive statistics, inferential statistics, models and simulations

Decision Support Systems

Although some see the decision support system (DSS) concept as no more than a management information system for complex nonroutine decisions, a decision support system contains some subtle differences that are worth noting. The focus of a management information system is to provide information for management decisions. The focus of a decision support system is on developing a flexible, interactive, and conversational data base that a manager can query in the language or logic of his or her profession. A management information system is frequently designed to replace managerial decision making by providing an optimum solution based on sophisticated analysis of data—for example, linear programming, modeling, and simulation. A decision support system is designed to support the manager's efforts to examine a variety of data in as many ways as possible in order to arrive at a decision. A management information system presents information in a format and style appropriate for the managerial level of the user. A decision support system leaves the style up to the manager interacting with the system (Keen & Morton, 1978).

Carlson (1977, pp. 5-6) lists four characteristics of a decision support system:

1. The ability to present information in ways that are familiar to managers and permit quick analysis of the data being presented.
2. A set of easy-to-use operations that can be invoked to prepare and transform the data or information selected for use by the manager.
3. Memory to retain the processes, the interactions, and the final results the manager goes through in arriving at the decision. This is similar to saving the scratch paper of a mathematician or rough drafts of a writer.

4. Giving the manager control of the operations usec
    to interact with the data base, for example, making
    it easy to select those operations, picking the ordei
    in which the operations are performed, and control-
    ling the memories.

Physically, decision support systems consist of four
basic components:

1. A computerized data base and a data base manage-
    ment system. As stated previously, a data base is a
    systematic organized collection of data that the user
    can easily manipulate and access. The data base
    management system is a set of software procedures
    that insures a well-managed data base.
2. An interactive time-sharing computer by which the
    decision maker can have immediate input and
    access to the data base.
3. A remote video display (TV-like screen) and key-
    board for decision makers to view the inputs and
    outputs to the data base.
4. A conversational software package that allows de-
    cision makers to communicate with the data base in
    the language and logic of their profession.

The concept of a decision support system holds much
promise for workers in human service agencies who must
make complex, nonroutine decisions on very limited data.
However, little effort has been spent on developing a data
base containing operational level data due to the problems of
quantifying the casework or therapy process and the outcomes of that process. Once a data base is developed, the
decision support system concept can be applied with substantial potential.

The following dialogue between a decision support
system and a child welfare worker has been constructed to

illustrate how a computerized decision support system could work in child welfare. This example has been dramatized to illustrate the capabilities of a decision support system. In this example, the computer has been programmed to pick up and use key words and phrases of the caseworker as well as to add predetermined dialogue.

CWSS: You are using the Child Welfare Support System called CWSS. Please enter your name and unique password.

Worker: Joe Smith, AZURE (the password is a coded key required to obtain access to the data-bank).

CWSS: CWSS can do the following 5 things to assist with your case decisions.

1. Provide a summary narrative on similar cases that were resolved successfully according to a panel of experts.
2. Identify key activities of cases similar to yours that were judged to have been handled successfully.
3. Compare the series of activities you are planning with your case and see what outcomes these activities achieved in previous cases.
4. Provide abstracts on many subjects related to your case. The system will search for the topic you specify.
5. Present the procedure for asking additional questions which can be answered by the information which is available in the system.

Type the number you want performed.

Joe: W

CWSS: The W entered does not correspond to one of the 5 items above. Please read the information above and type in either 1, 2, 3, 4, or 5. If you still do not understand, and if you have a question, just type HELP and our dialogue will be stored and a list of the instructions for

	using the system will be presented. Please type one of the above numbers or the word HELP.
Joe:	2
CWSS:	Have you filled out form 1045 on this case? Yes or No? [If "yes," the computer automatically gets the information from form 1045 and requests only the data missing or needed in addition to form 1045.]
Joe:	No
CWSS:	Joe, in order to perform the activity specified, background information is needed about your case. If you do not know the answer to the questions asked, simply press the carriage return key.
	Is there a father in this case? Press Y for Yes or N for No. [If "no," the CWSS automatically branches to the next series of questions.]
Joe:	Y
CWSS:	Is the father in the home? [Y or N]
Joe:	Y
CWSS:	How old is the father?
Joe:	37
CWSS:	What type of work does he do? [Press appropriate letter]

A. Unskilled laborer
B. Semiskilled
C. Professional
D. Other (For brevity, additional categories are not shown)

Joe:	C.
CWSS:	Has he been convicted of any crime? [If Yes, the computer branches to the questions which search for more detail, e.g., a crime involving aggression on another person or a crime involving drinking or drug abuse.]

Joe: N
          [Similar information would be gathered for
          the mother, household, family, etc., based on
          the variables that have been determined to be
          most relevant in abuse situations.]
CWSS: All the information needed has been collect-
          ed. Before reviewing similar cases, would you
          like Form 1045 to be typed from the informa-
          tion you provided and put in your files?
Joe: Y
CWSS: Form 1045 will be in your files tomorrow. A
          search of the data base has found the follow-
          ing information:

1. Three cases similar to yours with up to 5 exceptions.
2. Five cases similar to yours with 5 to 10 exceptions.
3. Seven cases similar to yours with 10 to 15 exceptions.

          The most similar case is identical to yours
          with the following exceptions:

1. There is no grandmother in the home.
2. The mother has divorced and remarried twice.
3. The abused child's older brother was age 4.

          Do you want to continue with the most simi-
          lar case summary?
Joe: Y
CWSS: MOST SIMILAR CASE SUMMARY: The
          worker removed the children from the home
          immediately and placed them in foster care
          for 1 week. The father and mother were
          referred to legal services to obtain financial
          help and consolidate their bills. The parents
          were required to go to Family Services for
          marital counseling for three sessions the first
          week and one session per week for the follow-

ing 3 months. The children were reinstated in the family after the third week, and the older children were involved in the marital counseling every third week. The case was judged successful by the worker's supervisor because of the following:

1. The family unit was quickly restored.
2. Six monthly follow-up visits by the worker gave the impression that the major problems were being solved.
3. No future complaints were received by or referred to the unit for one year following the reinstatement of the children.

Do you want more details on this case (Y or N)?

Joe: N

CWSS: Do you wish to have a summary of the second most similar case displayed (Y or N)?

Joe: Y

CWSS: The second most similar case was identical to yours with the following exceptions: etc.

This example could have illustrated a therapist in a community mental health center or family service agency. The agency's data base could be queried to determine what therapeutic activities or modalities had previously been associated with improvement as indicated by areas of a global level of functioning scale.

Word Processing

Word processing, which emerged in the late 1960s, consists of computer hardware and software that collects, stores, edits, and prints the written word to the specifications of the user. A word processing system can perform a variety of functions such as

1. Rapid typing of original letters stored in the system's memory to persons on a mailing list in the system's memory.
2. Sorting and printing of mailing labels.
3. Text editing, such as automatic reformatting of margins, moving the position of text, and adding, deleting, or changing words or phrases line by line or throughout the total text.
4. Generating standard reports and documents.
5. Checking texts for common spelling errors.
6. Displaying several texts at the same time on a split video screen.

This list could be expanded, depending on the agency's computer and the software available.

Word processing systems are not focused on decision making but on automating the routine secretarial and writing functions. They vary by the functions offered, speed, quality of output, and reliability (Doliner, 1979). Word processing systems are a worthwhile addition to an agency computer and in some cases a microcomputer word processing system may be purchased on a cost-effectiveness basis, since it may prevent the need to hire additional clerical staff. For agencies whose communication is vital to survival—for example, fund raising of United Way—word processing capacity may logically be the agency's first computer application.

Word processing, although not usually considered an information management application, is being discussed because it is gradually being tied to other information management technologies. As Kleinschrod (1977) points out,

> The systems outreach of WP [word processing] is potentially so sweeping and its ability to interact with other office systems is so strong, that by the mid-1980s the true "integrated office system" could well be working realities in many American offices. They would fuse word processing, data processing, reprographics, microfilm, facsimile, and other telecommunications technology into one information support service. (p. 4)

In future office automation, word processing will be integrated with the organization's data base both as an entry terminal and as a "window" into the great electronic files stored within the organization's computer to provide such essential functions as electronic mail, office calendars, and files (Wohl, 1979; Wohl, 1980). It is one of the most cost-beneficial computer applications in the human services, especially for small agencies that generate numerous reports and mailings to their clients and the community.

Part II

THEORETICAL PERSPECTIVES AND RELATED CONCEPTS

Because the information revolution has spawned a new field of study called "information management," it is necessary to examine some of the relevant theoretical perspectives. The perspectives in Part II consist of theories, models, frameworks, and concepts that allow us to analyze and generalize about the field of information management. Using different theoretical perspectives for viewing information management is like using different colored glasses to view the world. Each color, or theoretical perspective, highlights and subdues different aspects of what exists. Each distorts the total picture as it emphasizes some particular aspect. The process can be compared to that used by artists such as Picasso, who used distortions and exaggerations to give us new insights into what exists.

Chapter 3

SYSTEMS THEORY, INFORMATION-COMMUNICATION THEORY, AND CYBERNETICS

Introduction

At present the major stumbling block in effective data management in the human services is not in hardware and software technology but in viewing the human service agency and the information it collects as a system and in applying the data and information generated by a computerized information management application in agency decision making.

This chapter defines systems theory, information-communication theory, and cybernetics, some of their most relevant concepts, and the implications of these concepts for information management. It ends with a description of a human service delivery system that illustrates and ties these concepts together.

Systems theory is a framework that is basic to today's information management efforts, for information management demands the logic, specificity, and interrelatedness characterized by the systems approach. Information-communication theory and cybernetics are more technical in nature, but they offer some valuable concepts that are essential to an understanding of the nature of effective communication and the role of feedback and control.

Systems Theory

Systems theory is a framework for viewing the world. Because systems theory is an approach or perspective applicable to all bodies of knowledge, its concepts are general and sometimes in unfamiliar language. Systems theory is also much easier to understand than to put into practice. To understand systems theory, it is necessary to understand the specific terminology associated with it—for example, general systems theory, systems thinking, living systems, open systems, applied general systems theory, systems approach, systems analysis, and so on.

People have viewed what exists as a system for thousands of years. It was not until the biologist Ludwig von Bertalanffy in the 1950s applied the concepts of physical systems to living systems, however, that systems theory began having an impact in the social sciences. A major tenet of Bertalanffy is that systems theory holds many analogies and isomorphosisms which apply to all living systems including organisms, groups, and organizations (Baker, 1974, p. 443).

A system, according to Bertalanffy (1968), is a "set of elements standing in interaction" (p. 38). General systems theory or systems thinking is

> A set of related definitions, assumptions, and propositions which deal with reality as an integrated hierarchy of organizations of matter and energy. General living systems theory is concerned with a special subset of all systems, the living ones. (Miller, 1976, p. 296)

Living systems are essentially open systems as opposed to closed systems. An open system interacts with its environment; thus an open system can be defined as

> A set of elements: (1) in mutual interaction, (2) characterized by an input and output in energy, (3) existing in a homeostatic state wherein its input and output will not appreciably affect its form, (4) manifesting an increasing complexity over time, and (5) displaying a high degree of interaction with its environment. (Herriott & Hodgkins, 1974, p. 123)

The following principles are the essence of open systems theory:

1. All parts in a system are interdependent.
2. The whole is more than a summation of the individual parts (synergy).
3. Parts can only be understood when the whole is comprehended.
4. Boundary relationships with other systems constitute important interfaces.
5. All systems exist in a hierarchy of systems.
6. Open systems are changing and adaptive.
7. Open systems experience growth and decay processes (entropy). (Carlisle, 1976, p. 107)

A system may be viewed either in structural terms—that is, as a set of interrelated elements—or in terms of its performance, particularly input-output activities (Stein, 1974, p. 3). The systems concepts presented here are of both a structural and a performance nature, and were chosen because they aid in our understanding of information management.

Applied general systems theory or the systems approach is the use of systems theory concepts and principles in an analysis. The open systems approach begins by identifying and mapping the repeated cycles of input, transformation, output, and renewed input that comprise the organizational pattern (Katz & Kahn, 1969, p. 103). The systems approach focuses on

1. The total system objectives and, more specifically, the performance measures of the whole system.
2. The system's environment: the fixed constraints.
3. The resources of the system.
4. The components of the system, their activities, goals, and measures of performance.
5. The management of the system. (Churchman, 1968, pp. 29-30)

Systems analysis is a specific application of systems theory in organizational settings and is defined as "the process of studying the network of interactions within an organization and assisting in the development of new and improved methods for performing necessary work" (Semprevivo, 1976, p. 37). Systems analysis consists of the following activities:

1. Problem definition.
2. Data collection and analysis.
3. Analysis of systems alternatives.
4. Determination of feasibility.
5. Development of the systems proposal.
6. Pilot or prototype systems development.
7. Systems design.
8. Program development.
9. Systems implementation.
10. Systems follow-up. (Semprevivo, 1976, p. 14)

Systems Concepts

The best way to understand systems is through an understanding of the related concepts. Each concept will be defined and then illustrated with a human service example and an information management example.

Subsystems and the Environment

A subsystem is a part of a larger system, and the environment is that which is outside the boundary of the system. If we define an agency as a system, a subsystem may be an inpatient unit or a child services unit and the environment would be the community, the state, and the federal influences in which the agency exists. The distinction between a subsystem, the system, and the systems environment is arbitrary and is used simply to designate what one is talking about. Each system is a subsystem of a larger system.

The importance of the concepts of subsystem and environment is that they help us see the influences inside and outside of the system. In implementing an information system our concern should not only be with the design and plans for the subsystem of the information system, but also with how the information system can become a functional subsystem of its environment, that is, the community of which the agency is a part. The definition of system boundaries is also important. For example, a traditional pattern has been to consider an information system as only the data processing function. The users were rarely considered a part of the system or even an important part of the environment. The system, then, was designed around data processing needs with little consideration of the user in mind. The result was often a well-designed system that was not used.

Boundaries and Interfaces

Boundaries are regions separating one system's components from those of another system (Baker, 1974, p. 444). The interconnections and interactions that occur at the boundaries between the subsystems are termed "interfaces" (Davis, 1974, p. 83).

In a human service delivery system the boundaries must be clearly defined. For example, letters of agreement between agencies specifying target populations, services delivered, and so forth, are necessary. Many of the problems a system experiences occur at the interfaces between two systems. Thus the concept of a boundary spanning role, such as a client advocate, is essential if the system is to be accountable for assuring that services are delivered to the target population in need. Boundary spanning activities are also necessary to implement an information management effort. Computer and systems specialists and human service specialists often speak different professional languages. The interface between the two professions is often mediated by a widely circulated written agreement of the jargon of each profession and a team that is composed of members of each.

Boundaries and interfaces are important in information management, because the problems arising when a modular information management system is put together naturally occur at the boundaries and interfaces. The problem areas will be where the subsystems fit together and in fitting the system into an existing organizational pattern. Clearly defined boundaries and interfaces are important for any future system changes; for as Davis (1974) notes,

> If a system is clearly bounded and its interfaces clearly specified, a change or correction may be made more easily than if it were imbedded in a larger process because it is easier to evaluate the effects of the changes or corrections and easier to test the alteration. (p. 106)

Hierarchy

Hierarchy, a concept analyzed by Kenneth Boulding (1956), refers to the differences in systems based on criteria as increasing complexity and abstractness. Boulding presents a hierarchy of systems ranging from static structures, such as geography and the anatomy of the universe, to transcendental systems involving the ultimates, absolutes, inescapables, and unknowables. Systems toward the highest level of complexity display self-correcting, adaptive, and learning properties (Van Gigch, 1974, p. 45).

The concept of hierarchy helps view social service systems in their environment or as part of larger systems. The concept of hierarchy helps explain the multiple and often conflicting goals so characteristic of many social service agencies. Goal formulation and definition takes place on many levels of the hierarchy, ranging from the clients to the staff, the board of directors, the funding sources, and the general population. Each level may define the agency's goals in a slightly different way, and each level's definition is an input for the agency.

The concept of hierarchy is relevant to information management in several ways. First, it presents a framework whereby complex systems can be divided into smaller and less complex subsystems and elements. Thus hierarchy helps us break down massive amounts of complex information into meaningful components for analysis, design, and for communication about the system to others. Second, breaking down a system into a hierarchy of subsystems and basic elements allows the development and implementation of the complex integrated system piecemeal, or one element at a time. Only with the concept of a total system can gradual implementation proceed with a minimum of major changes. Third, hierarchy focuses our attention on the relationship between an information system and the information system of its environment. An agency information system should be as compatible as possible with the information systems of its environment, but especially with those to which it is accountable, such as its funding source. This can be accomplished in several ways, for example, standardization of the definitions and format of the data elements, and if compatible computer languages are not feasible, data entry should be in a card image readable format to facilitate the transfer of data and information from one level to another.

Open versus Closed Systems

The distinction between open and closed systems is that an open system interacts with its environment, whereas a closed system does not. The point that needs to be made is that few systems are relatively closed. Most are highly dependent on their environment. For example, a human service agency that functions as a closed system and ignores professional and client associations, political activities, technological progress, the community, and other elements of its environment soon becomes stagnant, outmoded, and in jeopardy of forced change or closure. Similarly, a data base that does not reflect the agency's environment will be a constant problem for the agency.

Input—Conversion or Transformation Process—Output

A productive way to view any system is as an overlapping series of input–transformation–output processes. Inputs are the resources or start-up components that are acted on and changed by the conversion or transformation process into outputs, results, or outcomes. For example, Hasenfeld (1972) views a social service agency as a people-processing—people-changing system. People and human service professionals are the inputs and outputs, and service delivery results in their transformation or change. In an information system, the inputs and outputs would be multiple forms of information and data, whereas the transformation process would involve such functions as collecting, classifying, sorting, manipulating, summarizing, storing, retrieving, and reproducing.

Purposefulness or Goal-Seeking Nature of Systems

Systems are dominated and guided by their purposes or goals. Goals imply values, priorities, and scope and are the criteria for success. Part of the difficulty of successfully implementing information systems in human service agencies is the inability to define and quantify the goals and objectives of the delivery system. For example, there is no standardized operational definition of mental and social well-being, a goal often listed by social service agencies. The concept of goal definition in social services has continually plagued Congress, the executive branch, and others trying to manage and control the human service system. Our democratic form of decision making allows for multiple short-term and often conflicting goals. To develop a goal-seeking system is an extremely difficult task given our current level of goal definition.

Goals are relevant for information management, for unless a manager has clarity about his program goals and objectives and develops indices of success in reaching these goals and objectives, it is impossible to determine what data to include in the data base. One pitfall in implementing computerized information systems has been that agencies avoid or are not able to define their goals and objectives adequately to the computer programmers or system designers. Thus the designers or programmers must use their own conceptualizations of an agency's goals and objectives when designing a system. Many times the programmer's conceptualization produces an information system that inadequately addresses the needs of the agency. As Van Gigch (1974) has pointed out "the success of implementation strategies has been found to vary with the extent to which goals are 'operational'" (p. 303).

Optimization and Suboptimization

To optimize is to improve until the "best" is reached. In suboptimization, the best is reached on the subsystem level. The usefulness of the optimum and suboptimum dichotomy is apparent when one realizes that what is best for the total system is not best for the subsystem. Consequently, "only suboptima satisfy the total system objectives as well as those of the subsystems" (Van Gigch, 1974, p. 288). What is necessary in complex systems is concerted suboptimization or a continuous balancing of the objectives of both the subsystem and the total system.

It is eay to see how suboptimization is a problem. For example, a patient with a gunshot wound is brought to a hospital on Saturday night, treated, and released home to the same family feud, only to be shot again. No social services were provided the patient because the social service department was not open Saturday night. What exists is a hospital with an optimum surgery subsystem, yet a suboptimum social service system. The result is a system failure.

The optimum-suboptimum concepts help us understand the modular development of an agency information system. Care must be taken not to optimize one module at the expense of the total system. Rather than spend time optimizing one module, a new subsystem should be implemented. Only when all modules are implemented can the balance between optimization and suboptimization be reached. The same optimum-suboptimum balance must be reached in any distributed information system. The optimum functioning of each distributed system must be sacrificed for the concerted suboptimization of the total system.

Synergy

Synergy is the property of a system in which the whole is greater than the sum of its parts. We can see that the purpose of developing a community service delivery system is to achieve synergy. The effect of a community service delivery system is more than the addition of each agency in a nonsystem. In a community where agencies form a human service delivery system, clear interconnections exist between subsystems, and thus the client can easily go from one subsystem to another. Also the total system can track clients' progress across subsystems or agencies. Finally, if we view the community as a system, we can prevent suboptimization at the expense of the total system as in our present medical system in which we have optimized the hospital or treatment system and have neglected the prevention or community health system.

Synergy is also useful in understanding why an information services department is important. Data and information must be organized in a systematic manner before any synergistic effect can take place. As more complex procedures become available for changing data into information—for example, modeling and simulation—the potential synergistic effects of the data services department will increase.

Information-Communication Theory and Cybernetics

Information-communication theory grew up around the works of Claude Shannon of Bell Laboratories in the 1940s. It is an attempt to provide a unified foundation for the study of communication systems (Rosie, 1969, p. 145). Information-communication theory basically concerns the mathematical side of information and addresses such problems as quantifying the information rate, channels, channel width, noise, and other factors affecting information transmission. Information-communication theory has little to do with concepts of data acquisition, data quality, the flow of data through systems, its fundamental characteristics, and so forth (Schoderbek, Kefalas, & Schoderbek, 1975, p. 92). The theory was developed for communications purposes and its application to business and information systems has been of limited use (Davis, 1974, p. 34). Although information-communication theory is not directly applicable to information management, it has helped focus attention on information as a literal commodity and helped us understand the difference between data and information (Keen & Morton, 1978, p. 38).

Cybernetics is a difficult subject to define. Norbert Weiner in 1948 coined the term from the Greek work "kubernetes," which refers to the steersman of a ship. Weiner's original definition, which still stands today, was contained in the title of his book, *Cybernetics or Control and*

Communication in the Animal and the Machine. Although cybernetics has its base in the mathematical theories of Weiner, Claude Shannon, and Warren Weaver, today the tendency is to regard cybernetics

> either as a scientific umbrella of synnoetics (i.e., computer science and technologies, ranging from automation to the theory of programming), or as a philosophical approach aiming at synthesizing an enormous variety of sciences, both pure and applied. (Rose, 1969, pp. 9-10)

In a cybernetic system, there are three basic elements and three basic processes. They are as follows:

1. Elements: Detector, selector—transformation, effector.
2. Processes: Perception, decision making—processing, action.

When these elements are interrelated, a control or feedback communication loop is created permitting the system to control itself against some preset or dynamic condition (Weiner, 1978, p. 54). Cybernetics has greatly influenced work in computer automation, computer systems, and artificial intelligence.

According to Van Gigch (1974, p. 50) information-communication theory and cybernetics have had two divergent effects.

First, they have shown how social systems could be made to approximate the process of physical systems by the use of feedback mechanisms. From this perspective, they spawned rigorous systems theories of organizations which were analytical and mathematical in nature.

Second, they showed the impossibility of duplicating the features of automatic control that exist in living systems. From this perspective they spawned a less rigorous behavioral theory of organizations which combined the concepts of economic theory with the behavioral notion brought from psychology, sociology, and anthropology.

Information-Communication Theory and Cybernetics Concepts

Feedback and Control

Control in the management sense is "the series of steps a manager takes to assure that actual performance conforms as nearly as practical to plan" (Newman, 1975, p. 5). The central concept in control is feedback. Feedback is the communication with the control element that indicates how the controlled variables are deviating from the specified standards, Feedback occurs in two forms. Positive feedback reinforces the direction in which the system is going, whereas negative feedback reduces the probability that the system will continue in the same direction (Davis, 1974, p. 95). Positive feedback is not necessarily superior to negative feedback; the situation determines when one is more effective than the other.

The overall purpose of the control subsystem is to reduce the amount of uncertainty in the system. If the control subsystem is to reduce the uncertainty in decision making, then the feedback and the evaluation standard must be well defined. As Kahne, Lefkowitz, and Rose (1979) point out,

> Perhaps the biggest challenge in the control of a system is how to define the goal in a mathematical form that appropriately represents the desired behavior of the system and that can be evaluated from measurable quantities in the system. The task is particularly difficult in large systems where it is necessary to deal not only with the usual technological variables but also with social ones. (p. 78)

As a system changes from the mathematical and physical sciences to the social sciences, the control mechanism changes from a mechanical device, to a man-machine interaction, to a purely human control. For example, in a heating system, a thermostat controls the heat based on the standard of temperature. In a prison system, a guard and a locking door control access based on standard operating procedures. In a service delivery system, peers control the work of others based on some standard of service provision.

Figure 3-1 illustrates control in a human service delivery system. It points out the use of feedback in the control process and the relationship of control to other system components. The information system drives the whole process because in order to control the system, information on inputs, transformation, and outputs must be collected, stored, manipulated, retrieved, and fed back to the controller.

Flagle, Huggins, and Roy (1960, p. 63) point to three requirements for effective feedback control of any system:

1. The output of the system must be susceptible to quantification and measurement in order to obtain a definite discrepancy when comparing actual with standard.
2. This difference must be "fed back" to the effector and to the activity, in order to modify the input in each round.
3. The feedback must be provided without delays in order for the action and the counteraction to be relevant and timely.

Newman (1975) lists several guides in setting up a control system for repetitive operations.

1. Aim for stability and dependability.
2. Single out repetitive elements.
3. Establish normal performance.

Figure 3-1.   Control in a Human Service System

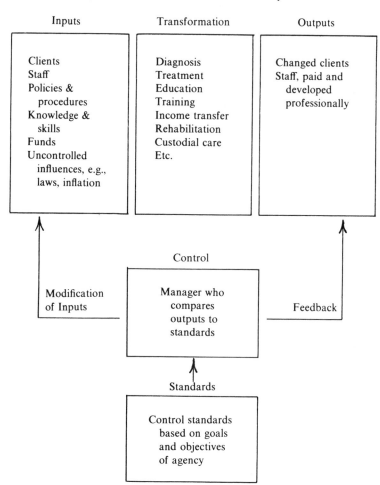

4. Retain an effective balance.
5. Simplify the controls.
6. Cultivate psychological acceptance.
7. Adapt to external variables. (pp. 49-60)

Control is very difficult to achieve because in complex systems, all the elements interact. Actions to control one input may affect another and the result may be the opposite of what was planned. For example, an information system can provide valuable information on therapeutic perform- ance that can be used to change inputs to improve the overall system performance. Information on individual perform- ance, however, can also cause fear and mistrust and result in a therapist resisting change by providing haphazard informa- tion that is impossible for the controller to use. It can also result in low morale and thus poor performance as indicated by increasingly negative feedback from clients.

Entropy

"Entropy," a term borrowed from thermodynamics, refers to the relative disorder, randomness, or variety in a system. Entropy is a major concept of information theory, since information theory is concerned with reducing the uncertain- ty associated with information transfer and outcomes (Singh, 1966; Pierce, 1961). Information in a system may be used to reduce disorder and uncertainty and thus reduces entropy. An effective management system provides the information that will help control the system and thus reduce entropy.

Redundancy

Communication theory points out the necessity of using redundancy to reduce message error. The transmission of redundant data and information allows a receiver to check whether the received message is correct, and, if not, the redundant information may allow this receiver to reconstruct the correct message (Davis, 1974, p. 40). The concept of redundancy is relevant to information management because of the low cost of providing redundant information. For example, many systems can easily calculate and print three measures of central tendency (mean, median, and mode) even if one or no measure is requested. Although redundancy in communication may be desirable, redundancy in data storage and in the data base is not.

Requisite Variety

> The law of requisite variety states that in order to control a system, a controller must be capable of taking at least as many distinct measures or countermeasures as the system which he seeks to control may exhibit. (Van Gigch, 1974, p. 377)

The importance of requisite variety for systems design is that it demonstrates the need for a method of obtaining a control response for every state of the variable being controlled. Because it is often impossible in human services to enumerate all possible responses, "The designer should consider enumerating the major cases in a decision situation and then use a supervisor or other person to generate responses to unusual situations" (Davis, 1974, p. 108). To achieve requisite variety requires precise timing and information on the major options in the decision situation.

An Illustration

The concepts of systems, information-communication, and cybernetics can be tied together and illustrated by the human services delivery system of Figure 3-2. This systems model of service delivery is being applied in several cities across the United States: for example, in Portsmouth, Virginia as described in Chapter 1 under service integration, and in Brockton, Maryland (DeWitt, 1977). From Figure 3-2 we can identify the following system components.

1. The service delivery, or operating system. This can be one agency or a consortium of community agencies.
2. The subsystems. An important subsystem of the operating unit is the data unit that contains the information system. The information system contains client records, tracks clients and their progress through the system; maps client pathways through the system; determines systems cost; and so on. The data unit furnishes the data that, along with the funds and people, drive the system.
3. The systems environment, that is, governance and the community.
4. The boundaries, interfaces, and interrelationships, especially of the system to the environment, as defined by the system's specifications.
5. The goal-seeking nature of the system or systems specification.
6. The control systems, which are the systems manager, the audit of effects achieved, and the governance.
7. The feedback loop, which provides information to the control systems.

Viewing the human service agency from the systems perspective is useful primarily because it helps us focus on ways to optimize or suboptimize within the system. As the designers of Figure 3-2 note,

> While perhaps no single element in this model can be viewed as especially unique, in the aggregate these elements comprise a system. And a system in today's world of human services is indeed unique! Remove any element from the model and the

Figure 3-2. An Agency in the Social Service Delivery System

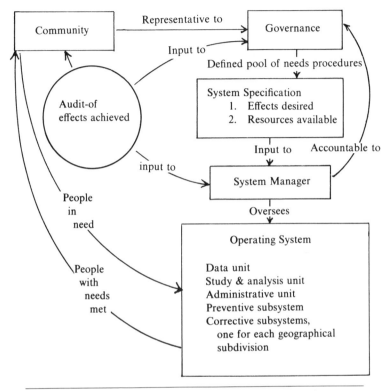

Note. From *Managing the Human Service "System": What Have We Learned from Services Integration?* by J. DeWitt, Department of Health, Education, and Welfare, Project Share, Human Services Monograph Series No. 4, August 1977, p. 83.

delicate balance that makes up a system is lost; the potential for productivity and accountability is threatened. (Mittenthal, 1976, p. 143)

Because the purpose of the system is concerted suboptimization of the system's goals, in this case defined as productivity and accountability, the designers have built certain characteristics into the system to insure that its movements are goal directed. These characteristics are as follows:

1. A client pathway that incorporates the critical functions (intake, triage, emergency, information, problem assessment, service planning, case assignment, maintenance, corrective service, follow-up) necessary for the delivery of positive effects on client need states.

2. A case manager who acts on behalf of system management to insure the reliable transit of a client through the system, and who serves as the single point of accountability for client success.

3. A data unit that provides both service delivery and management personnel with the information to insure client reliability (successful transit of the pathway). Such information includes a basic client profile, client effect and cost data, service resource inventory, and aggregate system performance data.

4. A study and analysis (long-range planning) unit that troubleshoots problems in the pathway, projects long-range system effects and costs, and identifies new service technology.

5. A set of direct service providers capable of delivering the requisite effects on clients.

6. A set of contracts that bind providers to delivering the effects specified by the case manager in the client pathway. (Mittenthal, 1976, p. 143)

We should note that systems criteria are often in conflict. For example, the criteria of efficiency, maximizing output from minimum input, and effectiveness or goal achievement are often in direct conflict. The system in Figure 3-2 is optimized around the goals of continuity and accountability, rather than the goal of reducing costs. A system designed to produce the same effect and also to optimize efficiency may look entirely different. A conscious process of balancing the optimization criteria is needed before a system can be designed.

Figure 3-3 presents one view of an agency service

Figure 3-3.   A Systems View of the Agency Service Delivery Process

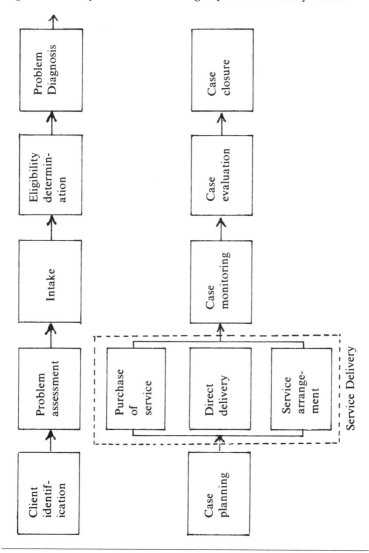

Note. From *Cultivating Client Information Systems* by G. E. Bowers and M. R. Bowers, Department of Health, Education and Welfare, Project Share, Human Services Monograph Series No. 5, June 1977, p. 10.

delivery system. A good training exercise would be to negotiate the optimizing criteria for Figure 3-3 and then show the interrelationship of the elements necessary to move the system toward its goal.

Concluding Remarks

The importance of the theories in this chapter is their focus on the whole and the interrelationship of the parts. These theories are not prescriptive, they do not tell us how to manage an organization or the information in it. Rather, they focus our attention on certain key areas—for example, the environment, interfaces, and control mechanisms—and give us general concepts for use in analyzing and applying these areas—for example, hierarchy and feedback.

Chapter 4

DECISION MAKING THEORY

Introduction

According to Rubinstein (1975, pp. 2-3) there are two approaches to research in human problem solving: the behavioral and the information processing. The behavioral approach, typified by B.F. Skinner, sees problem solving as a relationship between a stimulus (input) and a response (output) without speculating about the intervening process. The information processing approach, typified by Herbert Simon, is based on the information processing that accompanies the development of computer programs and emphasizes the process between input and output that leads to goal achievement. This chapter is based primarily on the information processing view.

In the introduction to this book, it was stated that decision making can be improved by changing the person, the organization, or the information surrounding the decision. These influences on decision making have been illustrated in figure 4-1. The decision-making concepts presented

in this chapter will be organized around the four variables in
Figure 4-1. They are

1. The decision or problem addressed.
2. The person making the decision.
3. The organization in which the decision is made or
   the context of the decision.
4. The information used to make the decision.

Figure 4-1. **Influences in the Decision-Making Process**

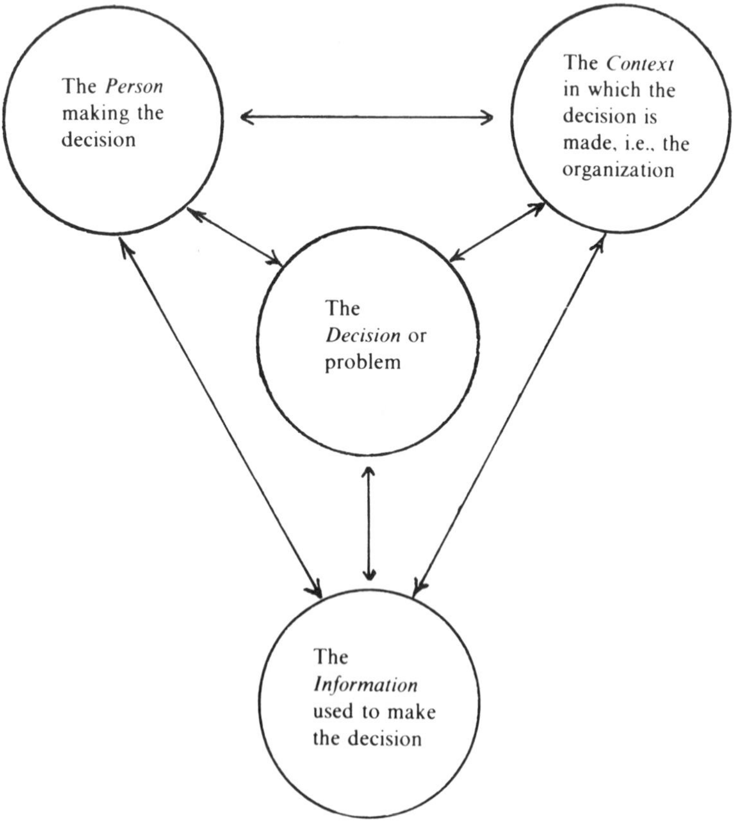

Before examining these four variables, it would be useful to examine the decision-making process. According to Simon (1977a) decision making involves four phases:

> Decision making comprises four principal phases: finding occasion for making a decision, finding possible courses of action, choosing among courses of action, and evaluating past choices. These four activities account for quite different fractions of the time budgets of executives . . . The four fractions, added together, account for most of what executives do. (p. 40)

One of the implications of the decision-making phases for information management is that different information is needed at each phase of the decision-making process (Davis, 1974, p. 141). For example, in a human service agency the first phase may require both general and specific information to allow for the examination of information in predefined and in ad hoc ways—that is, when a new client comes into the agency, the worker will want to see all the data and information available. Phase 4 on the other hand may require only information on preestablished indicators—that is, specific data on the client's change in functioning.

The Decision or Problem Addressed

Programmed versus Nonprogrammed Decisions

Simon (1960) distinguishes between programmed and non-programmed decisions. Each are at opposite ends of a continuum.

> Decisions are programmed to the extent that they are repetitive and routine to the extent that a definite procedure has been worked out for handling them so that they do not have to be treated de nova each time they occur . . . Decisions are nonprogrammed to the extent that they are novel, unstructured, and consequential. There is no cut-and-dried method for handling

the problem because it has not arisen before, or because its precise nature and structure are elusive or complex, or because it is so important that it deserves a custom-tailored treatment. (pp. 5-6)

An example of a programmed decision is welfare eligibility. In most cases welfare eligibility is a routine decision involving the comparison of client data with established criteria. An example of a nonprogrammed decision is the determination of the best mode of treatment for a client. Each client must be staffed individually, for each case is unique.

The relevance of the concept of programmed and nonprogrammed decisions for information management is that the type of information needed to support programmed decision making is totally different from that needed to support nonprogrammed decision making. Gorry and Morton (1971) point out that most decision-making techniques and skills and most information systems are designed to address the technical problems and decisions of a closed system, whereas most major organizational decisions are nonprogrammed decisions involving risk and uncertainty (p. 61).

Considerable disagreement exists on just what type of decision computerized information systems are capable of addressing. In a review of Herbert Simon's 1977 revision of *The New Science of Management Decision*, Mintzberg (1977) refutes Simon's contention that

> The processes of nonprogrammed decision making are beginning to undergo as fundamental a revolution as the one that is currently transforming programmed decision making in business organizations. Basic discoveries have been made about the nature of human problem solving and their first potentialities for business application have already emerged. (p. 345)

Mintzberg indicates that his own experience and the literature give little indication of advances in the solution of nonprogrammed decisions, and that "the more we look, the more complicated the process seems to be" (p. 346).

Although the academic debate will continue, two points need to be made. One is that few decisions in the human services fall on the programmed side of the continuum. The second is that the agency and the system designer should agree on the type of problems to be addressed. This agreement is not always an easy task. In a recent HEW project in which this researcher participated, designers and users spent two days trying to match problems the designers could model with problems for which users needed solutions. The task was impossible (Bergwall & Hadley, Note 1). Designers prefer to address problems that are repetitive in nature, whereas most problems that need to be answered by managers are one of a kind, unstructured, and high risk.

Certainty, Risk, and Uncertainty

Another way to examine a decision is to look at the decision maker's knowledge of the outcomes of the decision. Typically three types of knowledge with regard to outcomes are distinguished: certainty, risk, and uncertainty. In situations of certainty, the decision maker has complete and accurate knowledge of the outcomes of each choice. In situations of risk, all possible outcomes and the probability of each outcome occurring can be identified. In conditions of uncertainty, only several of the many possible outcomes can be identified, and little knowledge of the probability of each outcome is known (Davis, 1974, p. 143).

The Person Making the Decision

Keen and Morton (1978) describe several views on how people reach a decision. These views are summarized below, along with an additional one that is referred to as the "intuitional view." Each view will contain a simple illustration and a discussion of the relevance of that view for an information system.

The Rational View

In the rational view people seek out all possible alternatives, analyze and compare them, and then choose the best one. The focus of this view is on a rational comparison of all available facts. For example, a manager hiring a new employee would proceed by interviewing all potential candidates based on a set of prearranged questions, qualifications, and criteria usually developed from the job description. A manager would choose the best candidate and offer him or her the position.

This view represents the traditional or logical approach to decision making. The implications of the rational view for an information system are that the information system should present all possible facts and arrange the facts into new information according to specified criteria, for example, social indicators, models, and simulations. The information system must be organized logically and rationally and be able to present information backed up by a rational and logical analysis of data.

The "Satisficing" View

Simon (1945, p. XXIX) contends that administrators do not maximize—select the best alternative from all those available—but "satisfice"—look for a course of action that is satisfactory or "good enough." Thus man has "bounded rationality" due to the limitations on human processing capabilities. The focus of the "satisficing" view is on seeing only enough alternatives to find several that will satisfy the criteria of the decision maker. For example, a manager hiring a new employee may begin interviewing all those who apply, but cut off the interviewing process after seeing two or three good candidates for the position. The choice would then be made from these candidates.

The implications of this view for an information system are that decision makers can make good decisions based on limited information. As Appleton (1977) indicates

> The information required to satisfy 80–90% of management's decision making needs is, in most companies, developed from combining, arranging, analyzing, sorting, and reporting some subset of between 400–800 basic elements of data. From 400 elements of data, some 10^{869} different demands for output can be supported. (p. 87)

Because the decision maker uses primarily basic information, additional information has less and less impact. Once the basic information has been provided, a substantial investment would be required to improve the quality of a decision.

The Intuitive View

The intuitive view puts decision making into the realm of intuition, a hunch, or gut feeling. Data and information and all other influences are considered, but in the end the choice is one that "feels right." The choice may go against all reason, logic, and advice from others. The focus of this view is on making the decision by using the whole person. This view is sometimes seen as superior to using reason or other criteria alone, because the person is able to integrate all other information and holistically sense the best decision. For example, the manager may review all potential candidates and the job description and then go home, "sleep on it," and wake up with the decision made.

The relevance of this view for information systems is that flexibility is needed, and output from an information system should be in multiple formats to appeal to the whole person. The decision support system concept is most relevant for the intuitive decision maker who can test hunches on the data base; for example, the manager may want to know what additional skills would be needed if the organization expanded by taking on a new project. The intuitive decision maker would be able to use a data base that would answer "what if" types of questions.

The Organizational View

The organizational view sees decision making as basically rational, although highly influenced by established roles, procedures, and communications. It sees decision making as a series of influences of the formal and informal structure of the organization, its formal procedures, and its channels of communication. For example, the manager selecting an employee using the organizational view would examine potential applicants based not only on the job description, but also on the need to improve his or her status or role in the organization. The manager may hire the candidate who not only satisfies the formal requirement, but who in addition may be a beautiful young woman, a person with an impressive degree, or a person who has a particular expertise the manager feels may be needed to pull off a major power play within the organization. The manager may also interview from within the organization to gain favor with fellow managers.

The implication of this view for an information system is that it is very difficult to institutionalize an information system that does not take into account the informal organization and the coalitions of power within the organization. Trying to collect information that cuts across territorial boundaries and is inconsistent with the formal and informal structure, or with the established lines of communication, may cause resistance such as inaccurate or late reporting. The information system may attempt some integration, but usually at the risk of causing resistance.

The Political View

The political view holds that decision making is a very fluid process with multiple influences that are constantly changing. The focus is not on reason, roles, and procedures, but on power and influence within a context of multiple changing goals, values, and interests. Choices are not rational, but political. For example, the manager may leak word to his or her friends that a position will be open. The choice may depend not on the job description or the qualifications of those recommended, but on who recommended them.

The implications of this view for an information system are that information is an important political commodity. Who controls the information and who has access to it are as important as the information collected by the system. Design specialists frequently hold the rational view of decision making and develop the system accordingly. To counteract this tendency, a politically astute member of the organization should be part of the design team.

The political view is also useful in understanding why information generated by an information system may not be used in decision making. For example, the information system may logically indicate that one decision is best, yet the manager cannot choose that decision because it means firing the boss's son. The manager may realize from past experience that rather than firing the boss's son, the manager will be fired. Overreliance on information that is politically naive or neutral is as problematic as not using the information at all.

This view of decision making is very applicable to decision making in a community human service delivery system where decisions must reflect the politics of the individual agencies involved. In order for the information system to be accepted by the agencies in the community, it must reflect the coalitions of power and the traditions that exist.

Although the preceding five views of decision making are not mutually exclusive, we can say that a decision maker could be categorized as primarily using one view but having the capacity to use a combination of views depending on the type of decision, the time available to make it, and the importance of the decision. The argument is for flexibility and variety in the information system design and the ability of the information system to mesh with the decision-making style of the user. Keen and Morton (1978) refer to this meshing as the "individual difference view of decision making" (p. 73).

Most of the literature on the decision-making process focuses on the individual decision maker and ignores group decision making. The rationale seems to be that a group decision is a series or amalgamation of individual decisions rather than a separate phenomenon. The group as a decision maker, however, is used extensively in the human services— for example, staffing for the mentally ill, public involvement in planning, agency volunteer boards, United Way allocations, and so on. It should be viewed as a separate phenomenon.

One computerized information processing application organized around group decision making is called the "consensor" (Simmons, 1979). The consensor ties all decision makers together with a keyboard and video display. Each person can register an opinion qualified by five criteria, such as confidence in the decision, expertise on the subject area, enthusiasm, and power to implement the decision. The group's inputs are instantly tabulated by the computer and graphically desplayed anonymously to all participants. The consensor is designed to immediately point out areas of agreement and conflict and to promote discussion which will lead to better group decisions. Tied to an organization's information system, the consensor could be a powerful group decision-making tool.

The Organization in Which the Decision Is Made or the Context of the Decision

Many theories divide an organization into three levels of decision making or control: (1) operational or technical, (2) tactical or managerial, and (3) strategic. The focus at the operational or technical level is on the task to be performed. The focus at the managerial or tactical level is on the allocation of resources and the management of personnel. The focus at the strategic level is on the organization's goals and long-range strategies in relation to the external and internal environment.

It is easy to see how each decision-making level requires different data and information as well as different approaches to collecting, processing, and disseminating the data and information. Figure 4-2 points out these differences.

Fried (1977) by-passes the strategic, managerial, and operational categories because he believes that most information systems are falsely based on the assumptions of the

Figure 4-2. Information Requirements by Decision Level

Characteristics of Information	Operational Control	Managerial Control	Strategic Planning
Source	Largely internal ⟶		External
Scope	Well defined, narrow ⟶		Very wide
Level of aggregation	Detailed ⟶		Aggregate
Time horizon	Historical ⟶		Future
Currency	Highly current ⟶		Quite old
Required accuracy	High ⟶		Low
Frequency of Use	Very frequent ⟶		Infrequent

Note. From "A Framework for Management Information Systems" by G. A. Gorry and M. S. Morton, *Sloan Management Review*, 1971, *13* (1), 59. Copyright 1971 by *Sloan Management Review*. Reprinted by permission.

traditional bureaucratic model of organizations which no longer represent the ways most organizations think. Fried contends that information systems are usually structured to serve a centralized concept of the organization whereas in fact, there is a constant centrifugal force toward decentralization in any large organization. Information systems also usually move information up the bureaucratic ladder, separating and summarizing along the way. They rarely serve the equally necessary function of transmitting information laterally or disseminating information down the hierarchy.

Fried offers two alternative models of the organization, one based on Kurt Lewin's "topological psychology," the other based on Buckminster Fuller's concept of vector equilibrium. Both models define communication paths in such a manner as to by-pass the constraints of the hierarchical structure. They point to the necessity of controlling information resources and of establishing the shortest possible communication paths.

Even though Fried's ideas have not been substantiated by research, they point out the important effects that organizational context has on how information flows. They also point out that alternatives exist to the traditional information system design that can dramatically change the structure of the organization. Thus the decision maker and the system designer should agree on the organizational structure that exists or should exist and then design the information system accordingly.

The Information Used to Make the Decision

Use of Deterministic, Probabilistic, and Summary Data

Evidence suggests that serious deficiencies exist in human performance as an intuitive statistician. Man tends to handle probability data as deterministic data. This results in the following deficiencies:

1. Lack of intuitive understanding of the impact of sample size or sampling variance.
2. Lack of intuitive ability to identify correlation and causality.
3. Biasing heuristics for probability estimation.
4. Lack of capability for integrating information. (Davis, 1974, p. 71)

These deficiencies can be compensated for by a well-designed information system. The designer, however, must be aware of the decision maker's deficiencies and collect and display the data and information accordingly. For example, many managers by-pass less costly sampling techniques and continue to analyze total populations. If the information system is to produce sampling information, the level of confidence of the resulting statistics should be an integral part of the data.

Research on decision makers also indicates that they make better decisions with summary data, but are more confident of their decisions when they have raw data (Davis, 1974, p. 73). The concept of redundancy discussed in Chapter 3 applies here. Information systems should provide summary data for decision making and raw data for the user to scan to strengthen the confidence in the decision.

Value of Unused Data

Human service organizations tend to collect and store data that have little chance of being used. Psychological theories point to the comfort and value of this unused data for decision makers (Davis, 1974, p. 75).

The implications for information systems are that data based on the major decisions that must be made should be automated. A cost-benefit analysis, however, should be automatically conducted on any additional data decision makers request be put into the information system. At times it may be more economical to collect, store, and retrieve little-used data by hand.

Information Overload

As indicated by the concept of bounded rationality, the ability of humans to use large volumes of information in decision making is limited. With information overload, performance decreases with each new item of information presented.

The concept of information overload helps us keep in mind that humans cannot use all the data an information system can output. An example of information overload can be seen where large runs of computerized data and information are presented to citizen board members of human service organizations. What happens is that many members cannot comprehend all the input. They therefore refrain from participating in the decision-making process. Organizing and summarizing are two ways to reduce information overload (Cobb, 1977, p. 108).

Mode of Presentation

Although it is agreed that the computer is the best way to process information, the printout and video display may not be the best ways to communicate information. Little research exists on how the mode of presentation affects the use of an information system, but it obviously is a critical variable. Flexibility again seems to be important, so that a range of communication mediums can be used. This flexibility is becoming possible with the potentials offered by computer-generated graphics and charts, computer graphics, and animated simulations.

Concluding Remarks

Decision making, although the crucial process running through all organizational behavior, is a process about which we know very little. It has been an extremely difficult concept to quantify and analyze, since it is as complex as intelligence itself. The overall theme running through this chapter is the necessity of meshing any information management application to the variables in the decision-making process—that is, the information available, the decision being addressed, the organization, and the user. Information management applications, such as a decision support system, that appeal to the variety of states in each of these four variables have a better chance to be used. As the number of users and uses of information in organizations continue to expand, information processing seems to be moving into the more flexible concepts of decision support, in which the information system is useful no matter what the decision, the information available, the organization, or the characteristics of the user.

This discussion of decision making helps us understand why the decision support concept has relevance for human services. In human service organizations, both top-level managers and workers are usually faced with nonprogrammable decisions under conditions of uncertainty. Traditional information systems have not been able to address these nonprogrammable decisions and have thus been focused around the data of the more programmable decisions of middle managers, such as accounting and client data. For information management applications to be used by all human service personnel in an agency, the decision support concept should be used. Decision support, however, requires an operational data base, and human services have had extreme difficulty quantifying data at the operational or worker-client level, for example, data to indicate progress or success in a therapeutic or child abuse situation. Much work remains to be done in applying information management applications to complex decision making in human services.

Chapter 5

DIFFUSION OF INNOVATION THEORY

Introduction and Definitions

Diffusion of innovation theory is concerned with what variables are associated with the successful introduction of a new technology. Its relevance is in identifying the important variables that would either aid or hinder the introduction of a computer-based information management application into an organization.

The relatively young field of diffusion of innovation research has been rapidly expanding as indicated by the over 500 articles reviewed by Rogers in 1962 and the 1,500 articles reviewed by Rogers and Shoemaker in 1971. Diffusion of innovation research has been carried out in many disciplines, for example,

1. Anthropology: The diffusion of cultural traits among primitive tribes.
2. Rural sociology: The diffusion of hybrid seed corn among farmers.

3. Medical sociology: Drug adoption by physicians.
4. Education: Some 150 studies made at Columbia University.
5. Industry: The diffusion of a new product among customers.
6. Political science: The diffusion of city manager government in the United States.
7. Medicine: The contagion of a disease (Gray, 1973, p. 1175).

One branch of diffusion of innovative research concerns the organization as the unit of adoption. An examination of the literature on organizational innovation, shows organization theory and diffusion theory converging into a particular kind of organizational change—that associated with new ideas or a new technology. This chapter addresses one aspect of research on the diffusion of innovations in organizations. Specifically, it examines the variables that decrease or increase the probability that organizations will successfully adopt an innovation such as a computer-based information management application.

Organizational innovation research has taken on increasing importance over the years. Due to the demands of efficiency, productivity, and equity, decision makers are increasingly seeing the need for the ability to hasten or retard the diffusion of specific innovations. For example, the National Institute of Mental Health is presently funding research to examine what happens to an innovation once it is adopted in a community mental health center (Sustaining, 1976, p. 10). The end result of this research will be a set of consultation strategies and techniques. It is precisely this applied interest in the applicability of diffusion theory that seems to have dominated the research. As Becker and Whistler (1967, p. 469) indicate, it is rare that empirical work in organizational innovation stems from or relates to theoretical analysis.

Diffusion is "the process by which an innovation is spread through communication channels to members of a social system, for example, firms in an industry, over time" (Zaltman Duncan, & Holbek, 1973, p. 14). Adoption is "a decision to make full use of a new idea as the best course of action available" (Rogers & Shoemaker, 1971, p. 26). An innovation is "any idea, practice, or material artifact perceived to be new by the relevant unit of adoption" (Zaltman et al., 1973, p. 10).

The innovation process can best be seen in the context of models of organizational change. Diffusion research is related to any of these models in which change involves a new idea. However, it best fits the research, development, and diffusion model (Sashkin, Morris, & Horst, 1973). Two independent analyses of organizational diffusion of innovation (Rowe & Boise, 1974; Zaltman, et al., 1973), after examining three different models of organizational innovation, have postulated five similar stages to the organizational innovation process. These stages are

1. Awareness and accumulation of knowledge.
2. Formulation of a new innovation or attitudes toward an existing innovation.
3. Decision to adopt or reject the innovation.
4. Initial or trial implementation.
5. Sustained implementation.

When an innovation is diffused and adopted by a significant number of relevant units in a social system to register an impact and become an integrated part of the normative pattern in the system, the innovation process has been completed and it is said that social change has occurred (Zaltman et al., 1973, p. 14). When the innovation process is complete, theories of change management are appropriate.

With these concepts in mind, we can begin to examine what variables decrease or increase the probability that organizations will successfully adopt an innovation. One way to analyze this question to by first looking at the innovation, next the innovation process, and finally the adoption unit.

Factors Influencing Successful Innovation

The Innovation

Types of Innovations. Many researchers and theorists have developed typologies of innovations (see Fig. 5-1). These typologies, however, have not been tested and are presented here only as part of the theoretical framework.

Characteristics of Innovations. Only those characteristics and findings relevant to organizational adoption will be listed here.

The relative advantage over other innovations. Economic and social cost, return on investment, efficiency, risk and uncertainty, and multiple applicability are some of the characteristics. The findings are as follows:

1. The larger the number of critical attributes (those things the innovation does that other alternatives do not) and the greater their magnitude, the more likely the innovation is to be adopted.
2. The more amenable to demonstration the innovation is, the more visible are its advantages, and thus the more likely it is to be adopted (Zaltman et al., 1973, p. 39).

Communicability. The findings here are as follows:

1. The ease and effectiveness with which the result of an innovation can be communicated to others constitute a major force in the diffusion process (Czepiel, 1975, p. 85; Rogers & Shoemaker, 1971, p. 155).

2. The observability of an innovation, as perceived by members of a social system, is positively related to its rate of adoption (Rogers & Shoemaker, 1971, p. 156).

Figure 5-1. Types of Innovations

Types of Innovations in Terms of the State of the System
1. Programmed innovations
2. Nonprogrammed innovations ⎤   Knight 1967
   (a) Slack innovations ⎤ Cyert and
   (b) Distress innovations⎦ March, 1963

Types of Innovations in Terms of Their Initial Focus
1. Technological innovations   Dalton
2. Value-centered innovations et al.
3. Structural (administrative) 1968   (a) Ultimate ⎤
   innovations   innovation ⎤ Grossman
                               (b) Instrumental⎥ 1970
1. Product or service innovation ⎤   innovation ⎦
2. Production process innovations ⎥
3. Organizational-structural innovation⎥ Knight
4. People innovation   ⎦

Types of Innovations in Terms of Their Outcome or Effect
1. Performance radicalness⎤ Knight, (i) large scale⎤ Harvey and
2. Structural radicalness ⎦ 1967   (ii) small scale⎦ Mills, 1970

1. Variations (imply minor changes)
2. Reorientations (imply major changes)
   (a) Systematic reorientations ⎤
   (b) Idiosyncratic reorientations⎥ Normann, 1971
   (c) Marginal reorientations   ⎦

Note. From *Innovations and Organizations* by G. Zaltman, R. Duncan, and J. Holbek, New York: Wiley, 1973, p. 31. Copyright 1973 by Wiley. Reprinted by permission.

Compatibility. The findings are as follows:

1. "The pervasiveness or degree to which an innovation relates to and requires changes or adjustments on the part of the other elements in the organization influences the speed of adoption" (Zaltman et al., 1973, p. 37).
2. An innovation that is perceived as consistent with the existing values, past experiences, and the needs of the receiver has a high rate of adoption (Rogers & Shoemaker, 1971, p. 145).

Complexity. The findings are "generally, the more complex an innovation is in terms of operating, the less rapid its acceptance will be" (Zaltman et al., 1973, p. 38).

Trialability. Reversibility, divisibility, commitment required, and terminality are examples of triability. The findings are as follows:

1. The degree to which and the ease with which the status quo can be reinstated have positive effects on adoption (Zaltman et al., 1973, p. 45).
2. The degree to which an innovation can be broken down and gradually implemented has a positive effect on adoption (Zaltman et al., 1973, p. 45).

The Innovation Process

Research on the organizational innovation process is even more sketchy than that on the innovation. Little other than theoretical speculation exists. In most research we are fortunate if the author even identifies the stage of the innovation process to which the results apply.

One theoretical approach focuses on an organizational performance gap between what the organization is doing and what the organization ought to be doing. This model can be stated as follows: Adoption is a function of the expected value of possible outcomes, the variance of likely rewards through adoption, and the expectancy of achieving a target outcome (Dickson, 1976, p. 302).

March and Simon (1958, pp. 182-183) present another theoretical approach. In their model, innovations are sought whenever a given program of activity no longer satisfies performance criteria and a performance gap occurs. Their theory is that, over time, the aspiration level of an organization tends to adjust to the achievement level, thus reducing the performance gap.

March and Simon are more concerned with the initiation phase of the innovation process than with the implementation phase. In Wilson's work, which is discussed later in this chapter, the necessity of discussing both phases of the innovation process is pointed out, since they are radically different in many respects.

Jack Rothman and his colleagues (Rothman, Erlich, & Teresa, 1976, p. 7) have established four basic principles for innovation in the human services based on a 6-year research project. They are

1. Developing an innovation initially in a partial segment of the target system.
2. Changing the group structure in order to effect its goals.
3. Offering benefits in order to increase participation.
4. Increasing the effectiveness of role performance by clarifying the role and obtaining agreement about it among relevant superiors and influentials.

Although findings of Rothman and his colleagues are not surprising, their work is important, for it demonstrates the difficulty of testing principles of diffusion research in real-life settings.

Other suggestions related to the innovation process have been presented by Whisler (1970) and Carlisle (1976).

1. Choose a person who is trusted by both the experts (technicians) and by those who will operate the system to act as a go-between—for example, the county extension agent is a go-between between the technical experts in the universities and the farmers. This person must be able to communicate and understand both the experts and the direct service providers, and to communicate problems and advice up and solutions and interpretations down. This should be a permanent arrangement, so the stability of the person selected is an important factor (Whisler, 1970, p. 43).

2. The reasons and benefits associated with the innovation should be communicated to those involved as far in advance as possible. People will form their opinions and make their decisions on rumors if the facts are not available.

3. Protection should be provided for all those who will potentially be harmed by the change. Retraining and attrition is preferable to termination.

4. Those who go along with the change should be rewarded.

5. Change should be as gradual as conditions will permit. Evolution is preferable to revolution. Trial balloons (deliberate leaks) are a useful technique to get a feel of the reaction to or to warn of an impending decision. Structural change normally requires a minimum of 1 year to implement and test out; major changes in the organization require 3 or more years to reap the full benefits.

6. Where possible, those affected should participate in developing the change (Carlisle, 1976, p. 449).

The Adoption Unit

Most research on organizational diffusion of innovation has focused on the organizational climate that is conducive to innovation occurring. Although the organization has been the main focus, the adoption unit can also be seen as individuals and groups within the organization, the organization as a whole, and extraorganizational variables.

Individuals and Group Within the Organization. The innovative individual has been analyzed in terms of many leading theories—for example, motivation theory, dissonance theory, decision theory, and creativity theory. Baldridge and Burnham (1975, p. 175), however, found that individual characteristics, such as sex, age, and personal attitudes, do not seem to be important determinants of innovative behavior among people in complex organizations. Administrative positions and roles (that is, those who have power, sanctions, communication linkages, and boundary roles) seem to determine the involvement of an individual in the innovative process. Becker (1970, p. 267) found that a professional's innovativeness determines his centrality in the organizational communication network, and a desire to maintain or increase prestige motivates the professional to seek sources that are most likely to provide information on innovations. Corwin (1972) came up with similar findings, which stress the importance of roles and status in organizational innovation. He concluded,

> The competence, professionalism, and social liberalism of the rank-and-file professionals in the host organization were less important than either the comparable characteristics of the boundary personnel or the characteristics of the organizational structure. (p. 451)

Equally important as status and role are the interpersonal relations of the innovating social unit. Any organizational change, and especially change involving innovation, includes uncertainty and risk and produces stress, anxiety, and conflict among the participants. Stress destroys communication linkages and reduces performance. Thus a cohesive integrated social unit can be an important factor in the innovation process.

Havelock and his colleagues (1969), in a massive review of innovation-related research, found seven key factors (listed below) in knowledge dissemination and the utilization of knowledge for innovation.

Linkages, or the degree of interpersonal or intergroup connections. The more linkages that exist and the stronger they are, the more effective will be the information exchange and the greater will be the mutual utilization of knowledge.

1. In order for information to be successfully presented, the norms and cohesiveness of the group must be known.
2. If the innovation follows a course known to be acceptable to the group, the group will accept the innovation if the individual presenting it is himself acceptable or if the innovation is not presented in the context of other unacceptable ideas or innovations.
3. If an innovation is unacceptable to a group, special care must be taken to prepare the group to make it more susceptible to acceptance, for example, group discussions and involvement in the total process.
4. Initial acceptance by a small minority of key influentials is a major factor in diffusion to the community as a whole.

Structure, or the systematic organization and coordination of elements. Successful utilization activities tend to be structured activities and useful knowledge is structured knowledge.

Openness, or the readiness to give and receive new information.
Openness to help, listen, and take risks is essential to produce
the flexibility needed in the innovation process.

Capacity, or competence. Those who possess wealth, power,
status, education, intelligence, and sophistication are the
most successful innovators and utilizers of information.

Reward, or reinforcement. It is a fundamental psychological
fact that the rate of individual behavior increases if it is
followed by profitability, self-gain, or personal satisfaction.

*Proximity, or the chance to observe and stimulate one another
by reason of being in the same place at the same time.* Easy
access to information, people, and ideas promotes familiarity, acceptance, and use.

*Synergy, or the focusing of a combination of forces on a single
point.* A variety and redundancy of messages through a
number of different channels and with a number of different
formats are needed to achieve the adoption of an innovation
(Havelock et al., 1969).

The Organization.   Human relations management theorists
have continually criticized the Weberian bureaucratic model
and the scientific management concepts of Frederick Taylor
and Henry Fayol as restrictive for the growth of ideas within
the organization. For example, Shepard (1967, p. 477) advocates basic structural changes, such as project forms of
organizations or "senior scientists" with complete freedom to
create, as prerequisites to organizational innovation. Shepard
sees the need for a totally different outlook on life, on
oneself, and on others in order to foster innovation. He views
this outlook as less competitive and less oriented toward
money, power, and status.

The interaction between organizational structure and
innovation, however, seems more complicated than Shepard
and others recognize. James Q. Wilson (1966) contends that

high diversity leads to organizational members conceiving and proposing more innovations but not adopting these innovations. In other words, innovative and creative climates hinder concensus and decision making. Wilson's hypothesis has been supported by subsequent research, for example, Sapolsky (1967, p. 509).

The key to solving the dilemma is not to assume that the whole organization is characterized by diversity or homogeneity. In large organizations a diverse and creative climate should exist in units of the organization concerned with the initial phase of the innovation process, whereas less diverse and more bureaucratic units should be involved in the later phase of the process (Becker & Whisler, 1967). This solution, however, is not applicable to small organizations because small organizations may not be able to change their structure and climate depending on what stage of the innovation process they are in. In small organizations the director may adapt his or her administrative style to the innovation process by encouraging creativity, diversity, and participation during the initial two stages of the innovation process and exercising more control and structure during the final stages.

Several other interesting propositions are presented by Wilson (1966, pp. 207-214) as follows:

1. It is easier (less costly) to increase an organization's capacity to generate new proposals than it is to increase its capacity to ratify any given proposal.
2. Decentralization can be regarded as a method for increasing the probability of ratification of new proposals by confirming (in advance) their effects to certain subunits.
3. Innovative proposals will be more frequent in organizations in which a high degree of uncertainty governs the members' expectations of rewards.

As are Wilson's other hypotheses, these propositions are based on the view of an organization as either being diverse, and thus promoting the innovation, or as being structured and promoting the adoption of an innovation.

Recent views of organizations as being contingent on the situation are more realistic than Wilson's dichotomy. Contingency theorists see organizations as constantly adapting to the situation, and thus capable of being diverse at one point in time and structured at other points. Zaltman and his colleagues (1973) give empirical support to this contingency approach to innovation. They found that "decision-making units do alternate over time between flexibility and stability in structure in dealing with routine and nonroutine decisions" (p. 133). They go on to list several of the organizational contingencies that they see affecting the innovation process. These are complexity, formalization, centralization, interpersonal relations, and the ability to deal with conflict. Zaltman et al.'s general finding is that

> In stimulating the initiation of innovation, a higher degree of complexity, lower formalization, and lower centralization facilitate the gathering and processing of information, which is crucial to the initiating stage ... in the implementation stage a higher level of formalization and centralization and a lower level of complexity are likely to reduce role conflict and ambiguity which could impair implementation (p. 155).

Zaltman et al., conclude that an organization must shift its structure as it goes through the innovative process, and it must also develop integrative conflict-reducing mechanisms.

Another organizational variable discussed in the literature, but not supported by empirical evidence, is that both successful and failing organizations are more likely to be innovative than are those that are stable. The rationale is that successful organizations have the freedom to experiment whereas failing organizations must change to prevent their own destruction (Knight, 1967, p. 486; Wilson, 1966, p. 208). This finding seems to support March and Simon's (1958)

model which states that innovation occurs due to a performance gap. Knight, however, seems to imply a less gradual
process than March and Simon and that a substantially
larger performance gap is needed to produce innovation.

The Organization's Environment. Because organizations
are open systems, the environment plays a crucial role in the
innovative process. The environment here may be conceptualized in terms of the following influences:

1. Political and legal forces and institutions.
2. Technological forces and institutions.
3. Sociocultural forces and institutions.
4. Economic forces and institutions (Carlisle, 1976, p.
   60).

Zaltman and his colleagues (1973, p. 120) have identified
three types of information that the organization must obtain
from its environment for successful innovation:

1. The kinds of outputs the environment seeks that
   may require innovation to be more readily received
   by the environment.
2. The kinds of technology or means that may be
   required to produce the innovation (what the other
   organization is doing).
3. Once innovation occurs, the kinds of feedback that
   indicates the innovation is meeting the demands of
   the environment.

Most research on organizational innovation and organizational environments has been focused on interorganizational relations and communication. Milio (1971) believes
"Organizational innovation is best understood as a political
problem, one involving power relations among organizations

seeking scarce resources" (p. 171). Milio emphasized the importance to the innovation process of intervening variables that make for effective collective bargaining. For example,

1. Changes in customary relations as rule breaking and feigned compliance with prevailing bureaucratic procedures.
2. Formalization of a new nontraditional constituency and alliances.
3. The use of print media as a source of image building.

Milio's results help us see the situational nature of the innovation process and the power of environmental forces. Since she studied a government agency in conflict, the most relevant environmental contingencies were the political, legal, and sociocultural forces. Other more traditional organizations would probably be affected more by technological and economic forces.

Milio and others, such as Lin and Burt (1975, p. 256), point to the importance of communication with the mass media, the local media, and extraorganizational relationships. Czepiel (1975) found a functioning interorganizational communication network of friendly relationships linking firms together and active in the diffusion process. Czepiel concluded,

> The active use of friendship relationships in information seeking concerning the innovation . . . makes real diffusion a social process in the industry: the "social itinerary" of the innovation is quite clear. (p. 22)

Keeping up with the demands of the organization's environment and communication with friends, peers, and the media seem to be essential for successful innovation.

Concluding Remarks

In answer to the question of what variables decrease or increase the probability that organizations will successfully adopt an innovation, such as a computer-based information management application, all that can be said is that there is no single, clear-cut, across-the-board answer. The best answer involves a situational approach. Even though each situation is unique, the contingency framework examined can be used in all situations. This framework includes the variables associated with characteristics of the innovation; the stage of the innovation process; and the people, climate, structure, and environment of the adopting unit.

Much of the research presented on the variables in this framework is not surprising and seems to make good common sense. Rothman and his colleagues (1976) sum up the frustration that occurs after examining extensive diffusion research for applicable principles:

> These principles do not state startling, unusually sophisticated or esoteric ideas. Indeed, they appear to be quite commonplace and . . . are typically used by practitioners. . . . What, then, is the virtue of the extensive research process that proceeded formulation of the guidelines? Is this nothing but another example of social scientists rediscovering the obvious? . . . Research has demonstrated that many commonly accepted and widely used approaches are wrong. Urban renewal programs, instead of aiding intended beneficiaries, increase their misery. . . . When systematic research and practice common sense jointly sustain a strategy or technique . . . this is strong authentication that should not be taken lightly. (pp. 7-8)

Chapter 6

APPROPRIATE TECHNOLOGY THEORY

Introduction

"The history of technology is the history of invention of hammers and the subsequent search for heads to bang with them" (Drummond, 1978, p. 9). It is man's fascination with machines, regardless of their consequences, that has created the need for the study of appropriate technology. In one sense, this book is a study in appropriate technology, or how to apply computer technology appropriately to information management in human service agencies.

The intellectual catalyst behind the appropriate technology movement has been E.F. Schumacher and his major work *Small Is Beautiful* (1973). Schumacher argues that we should consciously guide and control technology rather than have technology guide and control us. He states,

> We can say that the modern world has been shaped by technology.... If that which has been shaped by technology, and continues to be so shaped, looks sick, it might be wise to have a look at technology itself. If technology is felt to be

becoming more and more inhuman, we might do well to
consider whether it is possible to have something better—a
technology with a human face. (p. 138)

The initial thrust of the appropriate technology movement has stemmed from the failures and sometimes disastrous consequences of the efforts of developed countries to
introduce mass production and large-scale technology to
underdeveloped countries. Only recently has there been
increasing emphasis, especially by low-income groups and
subcultural movements, on applying the principles of appropriate technology theory to developed countries such as the
United States. Congress has mandated the National Science
Foundation to establish a program in appropriate technology; and a small grants program in appropriate technology
was part of the proposed Energy Research and Development
Administration budget. California has an Office of Appropriate Technology that reports directly to Governor Brown,
who is a disciple of Schumacher.

Definitions

Appropriate technology is defined in a National Science
Foundation study (Note 13) as follows:

> A process of establishing social and environmental goals,
> evaluating the potential positive and negative social and envi-
> ronmental effects of a proposed technology before it is deve-
> loped, and then attempting to incorporate beneficial elements
> into the various phases of development and utilization. (p. 111)

Appropriate technology extends the productivity and
efficiency criterion of the traditional cost-benefit analysis and
considers environmental and social impacts as well. Assessing the impact of technology is important for human service
agencies because they are the systems of society that are

charged with treating many of the ills technology has created; for example, alienation and anomie, unemployment,
poverty, and so on. Agencies charged with curing the problems of technology should not be contributing to these
problems.

As we have seen, however, behind much of today's
efforts to develop computerized information systems in business, government, and human services, there have been the
goals of accountability and sound management, not the goals
that stress the social and environmental well-being of man.
Goals that promote social and environmental well-being are
troublesome in our society, for, in many instances, they are
in direct conflict with the goals of efficiency, productivity,
and maximized profits. We have discovered that what is good
for corporations such as General Motors and Exxon is not
necessarily good for the social and environmental well-being
of the individual or the country. The inhumane use of
technology, although efficient, productive, and profitable in
the short run, can be costly and tragic to the society as a
whole. The balance is delicate; appropriate technology is a
study of this balance and the premises that underlie the basic
conflict. The answer to this conflict is to develop technology
that is human as well as efficient and profitable, for technology is only a neutral tool; it can either be used humanely or
inhumanely.

This section will examine principles based on the use of
technology that foster the goals of social and environmental
well-being. Our experience with social and environmental
goals has not been as vast as our experience with efficiency
and productivity goals, thus the principles are not as well
developed.

Principles of Appropriate Technology

PRINCIPLE 1

The existence of technology does not require its use.

The existence of technology only requires that we examine what happens if we do not use it and others do, and the effects its use would have on our lives (DeMoll, 1977, p. 1).

PRINCIPLE 2

The amount of leisure time available trends to be in inverse proportion to the amount of labor-saving technology employed.

Technology is deceptive, for it is easy to see a computer doing the work of 10 or even 100 men, but harder to see that people in a computerized society work harder. Schumacher (1973, p. 140) discovered this principle when he lived in Burma, a country near the bottom of the industrial league. People in Burma had an enormous amount of leisure time available because they had less labor-saving machinery. They also did not experience the strain and stress of such highly industrialized societies as the United States, Japan, and Germany (p. 140).

PRINCIPLE 3

It is an injustice and at the same time a grave evil and disturbance of right order to assign to a greater and higher association what lesser and subordinate organizations can do.

The higher level bears the burden of proving that the lower level is incapable of fulfilling a function satisfactorily, or that the higher level can actually do a better job. For example, in an organization management will grow in authority and effectiveness only if the freedom and responsibility at the lower levels are carefully preserved. As a result the organization as a whole can prosper and be happier. Schumacher recommends establishing semiautonomous units within the organization and giving them the greatest possible chance for creativity and entrepreneurship. Each semiautonomous unit can be held accountable by a small number of weighted criteria, for example, profit. Management by exception, then, becomes a reality. Management's role is to direct, watch, urge, restrain, and, on occasion, demand. It focuses its talents on achieving a middle ground between preaching and instructing. One of its most difficult tasks is to carry through its creative ideas without impairing the freedom and responsibility of the lower formation (Schumacher, 1973, pp. 230-238).

PRINCIPLE 4

Technology once started is hard to control or undo. Appropriate technology is self-limiting and controllable.

Computer systems have a tendency to grow. What usually begins as a very small special-purpose system somehow becomes transformed with time into a medium-sized, general-purpose system. If a computer system is ignored after it is installed, it will grow, and a whole new set of management problems will appear (U. of Texas, Note 25).

PRINCIPLE 5

Appropriate technology is simple.

As McRobie (1977, p. 84) in an issue of *The Futurist* devoted to appropriate technology points out, it does not take a highly skilled person to make something that is complex, expensive, and labor saving. It takes a rounded, experienced person to be able to think his or her way out of the big technology trap and think in terms of small and simple. This is especially true of computerized information systems. Many clever and creative computer applications are so obscure and complex that not even the designer can explain them. Good applications are clear, understandable, structured, well documented, and consist of straight flows of logic and simple, comprehensible, stand-along modules (Philippakis & Kazmier, 1977, pp. 94-96).

PRINCIPLE 6

Appropriate technology conserves resources.

Resources refer to labor, money, energy, time, space, personnel, volunteers, client stress, and a variety of other inputs on which a human service agency operates.

PRINCIPLE 7

Appropriate technology encourages meaningful interaction with people.

Appropriate technology does not dehumanize, isolate, and cause anomie. One goal of an information system should be to foster communication that leads to better relationships within the organization.

PRINCIPLE 8

Appropriate technology serves the short- and long-term goals and values of the agency.

The ultimate test of a technology is not efficiency and productivity, but whether it improves goal achievement. The goals of many human service agencies, although hard to define meaningfully, involve delivering quality services to clients, and are sometimes in direct conflict with efficiency and productivity.

PRINCIPLE 9

>Appropriate technology frees and liberates.

Appropriate technology changes jobs that are routine, dull, and repetitive to jobs that are creative, meaningful, and rewarding. Job satisfaction is a major factor in social well-being.

PRINCIPLE 10

>Appropriate technology is difficult to achieve.

Appropriate technology involves taking the extra time and energy to predict the human consequences of technology and to minimize these by making the necessary adjustments or by choosing a more suitable technology.

PRINCIPLE 11

>Appropriate technology prefers to employ people rather than machines.

It is inappropriate to replace workers with a machine that over the long run costs just as much. We should not only consider the cost to the organization, but the cost to society if the displaced person becomes indigent and dependent. Many organizations are willing to let the taxpayer pay hundreds of dollars, so they can save $5.

Unemployment of those lacking technical skills is a major social problem which human services are trying to eliminate, not contribute to. We must retrain rather than displace people.

PRINCIPLE 12

>Appropriate technology prefers locally produced items.

Even with present communication capacity, distance depersonalizes and increases energy is needed to make up for the distance.

PRINCIPLE 13

Appropriate technology is repairable and expandable.

Recycling of human and physical resources is preferred to a throw-away mentality.

Concluding Remarks

Appropriate technology theory helps us become aware of the necessity of considering the impact on individuals as a criteria for choosing and designing an information management application. If an application is chosen because it increases agency efficiency and reduces staff, the agency should make a special effort to insure that it is not sacrificing the individual or overall goal achievement. For it is especially easy to become wrapped up in the potentials of information-management gadgetry and lose sight of the principles of simplicity, humaneness, and appropriateness.

Part III

KNOWLEDGE DERIVED FROM EXPERIENCE

Part III examines the experiences of business, local government, and human services with information management. Each chapter in Part III will give an overview of information management in one of these organizational settings and then discuss considerations in the preimplementation, implementation, and postimplementation stages of developing any information management effort.

Business organizations have the most experience, and these efforts along with limited research have been widely reported in journals and books. Local governments have had considerable experience in using computerized information to aid in providing city and county services and in generating information for policy-level decision making. Local governments experience more environmental influences than most businesses, for example, community boards, civil service, changes due to politics, and loss of elections. Because many problems and services of local government are similar across the United States, they have had more experience in technology transfers and the use of modeling and simulations. Human services' experience with information management has been primarily limited to the federal and state levels. Few information management efforts have been attempted at the community level due to the fragmentation of the present human services system and at the agency level primarily due to cost.

Terminology differs in the three organizational settings. The information management experience that predominates the business and human services literature goes under the generic term of "management information systems" (MIS), whereas the experience predominating the local government literature is usually referred to as "electronic data processing" (EDP) or simply "data processing" (DP). An attempt has been made to standardize terminology wherever possible, but in some cases standardization was either misleading or impractical. For the purposes of Part III, we can consider the following terms synonymous: electronic data processing, management information systems, and computerized information management. All refer to the process of collecting, storing, manipulating, retrieving, and reporting data and information for the purpose of improving decision making.

Chapter 7

THE EXPERIENCE OF BUSINESS

Overview

Since the first computer for business applications was installed in 1954, computer-based information applications have grown at an exponential rate. The first uses were single, unrelated applications at the lower levels of the organization and involved the automation of routine and repetitive clerical tasks. From this early beginning, applications began to proliferate into such routine areas as inventory and payroll. The computer's major value was seen as processing speed, improved efficiency, and displacement of clerical personnel.

In the 1960s, the computer's potential for managing information higher in the organization was recognized. The development of separate data bases and programs to monitor and control many organizational processes and to provide information on many mid-level management functions became common. Toward the latter half of the 1960s, the necessity for integrating these diverse data bases into an organizational data base became evident. The application-by-application approach was abandoned for a central system that would serve several organizational functions. By the late 1960s, information was beginning to be seen as a resource basic to the organization (Matthews, 1976, p. 7). This changing use of computers in the late 1960s was greatly aided by the rapidly declining cost in computer hardware and by the benefits associated with a fully integrated information system.

In the 1970s, the trend continued with more sophisticated data base management software and more sophisticated applications. The major change in the 1970s was the move to support decisions higher and higher in the organization and the dispersion of the data processing function throughout the organization due to the low cost of mini- and microcomputer technology. As this continues to occur, organizations move into what is sometimes called an information environment, where information management is the central function tying the organization together and the information system becomes a communication model of the organization.

Nolan (1979) in researching over 40 companies, developed a picture of the growth stages of data processing that a company goes through. It is surprisingly similar to the chronological overview of information management just described. Nolan's stages of data processing are as follows.

Stage 1.   Initiation:
Automation of several low-level operating systems begins in a functional area, typically accounting.

Stage 2.   Contagion:
Automation is expanded into operational systems. Emphasis is on innovation and extensive applications. Overoptimism and overuse result in a system that is overloaded, out of control, and inadequately designed.

Stage 3.   Control:
Emphasis is shifted from managing the computer to managing the organization's data.

Data base concepts and internal planning and control are introduced. The data management function is redesigned, formalized, professionalized, centralized, and elevated in the organization. User accountability is demanded.

Stage 4. Integration:
Rebuilding is completed. The system grows rapidly as it moves out to the user. Interactive terminals are used. Control is initiated by setting priorities for services.

Stage 5. Data administration:
Rapid growth again creates problems. A data administrator is hired and the function is moved higher in the organization. Growth occurs in microcomputers and individual computing.

Stage 6. Maturity:
System matures, all applications are completed. A balance exists between use and control, central and distributed processing, and so on. The system mirrors the organization's data flow.

Nolan's stages are extremely useful for helping an organization identify what stage of information management it is in and what growth lies ahead. Figure 7-1 presents the benchmarks and the expenditures associated with each growth stage.

This overview of information management in business should not lead one to believe that information management did not exist before the invention of the computer. Ross (1976, pp. 5-8) describes the evolution of an information system by examining the changes in information requirements from a typical small business, such as a neighborhood grocery store, to the requirements of a large complex organization. He aptly points out that the functions of management—that is, planning, organizing, staffing, directing, and

Figure 7-1. Benchmarks of the Six Stages of Data Processing

		Stage 1 Initiation	Stage 2 Contagion	Stage 3 Control	Stage 4 Integration	Stage 5 Data administration	Stage 6 Maturity
First-Level Analysis	DP expenditure benchmarks	Tracks rate of sales growth	Exceeds rate of sales growth	Is less than rate of sales growth	Exceeds rate of sales growth	Is less than rate of sales growth	Tracks rate of sales growth
	Technology benchmarks	100% batch processing	80% batch processing; 20% remote job entry processing	70% batch processing; 15% data base processing; 10% inquiry processing; 5% time-sharing processing	50% batch and remote job entry processing; 40% data base and data communications processing; 5% personal computing; 5% minicomputer and microcomputer processing	20% batch and remote job entry processing; 60% data base and data communications processing; 5% personal computing; 15% minicomputer and microcomputer processing	10% batch and remote job entry processing; 60% data base and data communications processing; 5% personal computing; 25% minicomputer and microcomputer processing
Second-Level Analysis	Applications portfolio	There is a concentration on labor-intensive automation, scientific support, and clerical replacement.		Applications move out to user locations for data generation and data use.		Balance is established between centralized shared data/common system applications and decentralized user-controlled applications.	
	DP organization	Data processing is centralized and operates as a "closed shop."		Data processing becomes data custodian. Computer utility established and achieves reliability.		There is organizational implementation of the data resource management concept. There are layers of responsibility for data processing at appropriate organizational levels.	
	DP planning and control	Internal planning and control is installed to manage the computer. Included are standards for programming, responsibility accounting, and project management.			External planning and control is installed to manage data resources. Included are value-added user chargeback, steering committee, and data administration.		
Level of DP expenditures →	User awareness	Reactive: End user is superficially involved. The computer provides more, better, and faster information than manual techniques.		Driving force: End user is directly involved with data entry and data use. End user is accountable for data quality and for value-added end use.		Participatory: End user and data processing are jointly accountable for data quality and for effective design of value-added applications.	

Note. From "Managing the Crisis in Data Processing" by R. L. Nolan, *Harvard Business Review*, 1979, *57*(2), 117. Copyright 1979 by *Harvard Business Review*. Reprinted by permission.

controlling—have remained the same, while the information to support these functions has changed dramatically. This change has been due to the increase in the size and complexity of modern organizations, especially the increase in the complexity of the organization's environment. Traditional information management efforts are no longer adequate to compete in this rapidly changing complex environment.

The phenomenal growth of information management in business has not been smooth. This will be evidenced by the following discussion of the major considerations usually associated with the preimplementation, implementation, and postimplementation phases of application development. It would be advantageous to analyze the business experience in each of Nolan's six stages, but, at present, the preimplementation, implementation, and postimplementation categorization is as sophisticated a division as most writings will allow.

Considerations Developed from the Experience of Business

Preimplementation

Perhaps the most crucial consideration in information management is cost. What should be considered in a cost-benefit analysis? In many organizations a totally new system of operating must be implemented rather than merely computerizing an existing system. Thus costs are highly dependent on an organization's present level of systems development. If an organization is already willing to spend money on implementing more systematic data collection procedures, then the additional cost of implementing a computerized system may be minimal and prevent the necessity of redesigning the system in the future. Besides obvious costs—such as personnel changes, training, computer hardware and software, maintenance and supplies, and office space and storage equipment—many hidden costs exist, such as the disruption of services and the conflict due to change. Costs also vary by what stage of information management the organization is in, as the curve in Figure 7-1 indicates.

Benefits are equally hard to measure. For example, it is hard to put a dollar value on improved efficiency, more accurate and reliable data and information, greater control, less paper work, staff reduction, and so on. Thus the basic costs and benefits are almost impossible to measure and we are left to expert opinion.

The experts, however, provide little help. The answer seems lost in endless debate with few experts qualifying their opinions by the type of application, the stage of development, or any other of the major crucial variables that influence costs and determine benefits. For example, Hanold (1972), responding to an article in the *Harvard Business Review*, stated that "Theoreticians may debate the topic fruitlessly, but a management information system has become an absolute necessity for successful operation of a large and complex business enterprise" (p. 65). A study by Lucas in 1975 (p. 918), however, found only a weak association between users of an information system and their subsequent performance, and he questions whether the heavy investments in information systems are justified. Fried (1977) stated that "when an MIS was confined to a single organization, it was, in fact, very successful. The most prominent failures occurred when an MIS crossed organizational boundaries" (p. 30). Murdick and Ross (1975, pp. 540-541) point out that most companies which have used the computer to automate routine clerical functions have been satisfied with the results and are moving toward improved systems for management application.

The question seems far from being answered. As yet, no generally applicable cost-benefit scheme that identifies and quantifies the major costs and benefit variables in an organizational information management application has been developed. We can assume that as computer hardware costs go down and experience improves system design, we can move more and more to the conclusion that information management is becoming worth the money invested. What still seems to be a problem is that the effects of many information management applications are overpromised and oversold. This overpromising results in high expectations that are not fulfilled, thus resulting in disappointment and dissatisfaction.

Tomeski (1969) and others present additional questions and concerns to be addressed in the preimplementation phase:

1. In what ways are present ways of doing things unsatisfactory?
2. Could noncomputerized processes be used if current methods were substantially improved? Is it feasible to improve present methods without computerizing?
3. What new needs exist that could not be handled by a noncomputerized system (Tomeski, 1969, p. 56)?
4. "No MIS should ever be installed unless the managers for whom it is intended are trained to evaluate and hence control it rather than be controlled by it" (Ackoff, 1967, p. 153).

Another concern is how to approach the implementation effort. Tomeski (1969, pp. 92-94) recommends an evolutionary approach that introduces controlled change over a limited span. He feels that converting exactly what is being done now to a computer implies that the current system is satisfactory and may be indicative of a conservative executive who cannot cope with change. Completely changing what is being done now implies nothing is presently effective and leads to chaos and high start-up costs. Horton (1977) agrees:

> Another admonishment we might keep close by is the need to take a careful, slow, and incremental approach to the design, development, testing, and evaluation of the system and approaches being advanced. Too many large data systems are still developed on some "grand design" blueprint which, it later turns out, is unrealistic, overly ambitious, too costly, and obsolete by the time the switches are pulled. This lesson has been a particularly bothersome and persistent one to learn; but it is one, nevertheless, that must be learned. (p. 9)

Neu (1976, p. 38) points to another concern. He states that the factor posing the greatest risk of all to the small company (25 to 100 persons) is its long-term dependence on one individual as the very core of its development effort. The risk of this one person changing jobs or positions is substantial considering the mobility of design personnel and the fact that some 2 years is required to demonstrate any benefits of a management information system development effort. Neu (1976, p. 37) also points out that the designer of a management information system must be more a manager than a technician.

Implementation

Once the decision has been made to implement an information management application, the implementation phase can be divided into the following stages (Barnett, 1978, p. 54).

1. Initiation and forming of the systems team.
2. Definition of the problem to be addressed, the requirements imposed by the users and others such as funding sources, and the opportunities that exist to maximize the system.

3. Conceptual-level design.
4. Description of the existing system.
5. Detailed design.
6. Design of all specifications and additional details.
7. Programming and testing and user training.
8. Conversion from present system to new system.
9. Operation and evaluation.

There is unanimous agreement that the key to successful implementation and future use of an information management system is the involvement of the user in all stages of the process. Barnett's (1978, pp. 53-54) discussion of the design team makes several important points that can help assure user involvement. First, the design team should be composed of different departments and offer a communication channel to all members of the organization. Second, its relationship with top management should be clear. Third, it should have clearly defined responsibility, such as sign-off capacity at certain stages of the implementation process (Stages 2, 3, 5, 6, 7, and 8).

Carper (1977, pp. 48-49) outlines sources of resistance and how to overcome them. Major sources include

1. Threats to one's status, power, ego, and economic security.
2. Feelings of insecurity, uncertainty, and unfamiliarity.
3. Perceived changes in job complexity, job rigidity, and job-role ambiguity.
4. Changes in superior-subordinate interpersonal relations and work patterns.

To overcome resistance Carper (1977, pp. 48-49) recommends

1. Establishing and communicating objectives.
2. Developing user involvement and orientation.

3. Involving top management.
4. Preconditioning employees to change as a normal part of organizational growth.
5. Considering the social and political consequences.
6. Maintaining open communication.

Murdick and Ross (1975, pp. 549-550) found five major sources of system difficulties based on a review of the literature, research studies, and personal observation. They concluded all could be overcome to some extent by appropriate top-management involvement. These sources follow.

1. Computer rather than user orientation. This reflects the use of the computer for clerical processing applications rather than for managerial decision making. As computers come of age, the orientation must change from record-keeping functions to those concerned with operational improvement.
2. Improper definition of user requirements.
3. Organization of the systems function. Traditionally, computer organizations were placed under an accounting or financial manager because of the "most use" principle. The successful company, however, places the overall responsibility near the top and involves operating management in increasing the effectiveness of the computer operation.
4. Overlooking the human side of information systems. Human fears and natural reluctance to change must be overcome with better communications regarding the nature, the purpose, and the impact of the computer.
5. Understanding complexity and costs. Unless there is adequate experience on which to base estimates, the likely tendency is to underestimate the cost and complexity of systems design and implementation. Accurate costing in the initial phase is critical because it frequently sets the mood and the course for the future.

Another major concern in the implementation phase is the involvement of top management. As Tomeski (1969) points out, "Almost invariably, any highly successful computer effort has had strong and continuous backing fom top management" (p. 88).

The involvement of top management may be more difficult than one anticipates. Whisler (1970) notes that problems of adoption multiply as system development moves higher in the organization.

> Clerks may offer passive resistance ... but the fact is they are accustomed to having things imposed on them. When one moves up to the supervisory and managerial levels, one encounters men who are accustomed to having some autonomy and authority in making decisions. Imposition of change at these levels causes difficulties of a much higher magnitude .... The potential for ... resisting new ideas certainly rises in proportion to the authority and power of those behaving in such fashion. (p. 40)

Burack and Sorensen's (1976) research indicates that the inability of management to cope or capitalize on computer capabilities exists because management's computer preparation often lags far behind installation, is narrowly conceived, is incomplete, or may never even take place. They conclude that

> Greater attention needs to be given to adequate management development policies and strategies in connection with the introduction of new technologies. Specifically, higher priority needs to be given to the assignment of responsibility for computer-related management education and the acquisition or development of adequate resources for the accomplishment of that task. (p. 322)

The necessity of adequate planning is a theme running throughout most implementation literature. Appleton (1979a,

p. 182) lists five acid test questions which, if answered in the affirmative, indicate a successful systems plan.

1. Were the objectives of the manufacturing systems plan derived from a good long-range business plan?
2. Was the systems plan constructed based on a comprehensive manufacturing systems model rather than being developed completely from scratch?
3. Does the system plan separate systems planning from planning for automation, recognizing that though all automated systems are indeed systems, all systems are not necessarily automated?
4. Does the plan integrate the traditionally separate worlds of technical computing and business data processing?
5. Does the manufacturing systems plan use a functional (data base) approach to automation, instead of an applications approach, to provide a flexible automated systems structure?

Another concern is that of selecting a systems manager. Neu (1976) indicates that in small firms "It is highly likely that the 'wrong person' will be selected to head up the MIS development effort" (p. 37). Because hiring a systems manager is a first-time experience for many small firms and an extreme shortage of qualified candidates exists in today's marketplace, Neu (1976, p. 38) recommends considering the use of outside expertise in interviewing and the involvement of operating management and top management. He advises that a business-oriented problem solver is preferred to a technical wizard.

Several other concerns deserve mentioning. The first is that many small commercial minicomputers allow for only a few data entry terminals, resulting in a bottleneck in the timely flow and processing of information (Neu, 1976, p. 37). The second is that a key element in the maintenance contract is the rapid repair of down equipment (Piecewicz, 1977, p. 15). Last, the attempt to refine or customize packaged software systems should be avoided. "Such refinements typically do not lead to materially more effective management reporting in areas where several software packages already exist" (Rittersbach, 1975, p. 112).

Postimplementation

The impact of computerized information management is probably as significant as any single development in business history. "It has caused increased reappraisal of many classical notions about the functions of management and the elements of business" (Tomeski, 1969, p. 88). Thus the obvious effect of an information management application on an organization is a reappraisal of its present operations, policies, and processes.

Job content is changed to some extent. Clerical jobs become fewer and more routinized while supervisory jobs tend to increase and move toward enlargement (Whisler, 1970, p. 124). The most common effect during the 2-year implementation period is an increase in the manager's work load (Stewart, 1971, p. 220). Duplication of normal duties may be required while the new system is phased in and the old system phased out.

One of the results of an information system is that decision making becomes less flexible as new information forces decision making to be increasingly quantified and rationalized. Also, decision making becomes centralized and moves higher in the organization, since better data make decisions harder and more complicated. Overall, computerized information systems seem to change the nature of the problems that decision makers must solve rather than provide solutions to them (Stewart, 1971, p. 336). Computerized information systems can also cause a tightening of control or discipline with respect to individual behavior, especially at lower levels in an organization (Whisler, 1970, pp. 93 and 124).

Computerized information influences organizational structure by causing a tendency to shift parallel departments to functional departments, since more control is able to be exercised from the top. Thus computers allow management to increase specialization if it is desired (Whisler, 1970, p. 63).

Some of the effects listed above must be viewed with a note of caution since they were published around 1970 (Lucas, 1978, pp. 59-66). The introduction of minicomputers and distributed systems could dramatically alter what has happened in the past.

Chapter 8

THE EXPERIENCE OF LOCAL
GOVERNMENTS

Overview

The dependence of local governments on data processing was forcefully brought to mind during a recent ice storm when the radio announced the closing of all but the essential functions of Dallas County, Texas. The only two services that were listed as essential were the county sheriff's department and data processing.

The demands and problems facing local government have increased dramatically since the early 1960s. As local governments expanded to meet these demands, they were faced with complex solutions and the need for accurate and timely information on which to make decisions and exercise controls. Compounding this situation is the fact that available funds have not kept up with increasing demands.

Under these strained conditions, data processing has been sold as a tool no local government should be without. This selling was aided by the computer's amazing ability to analyze and synthesize large quantities of data quickly, accurately, and consistently, and by the fact that little empirical research is available with which to evaluate the success stories and promotional information the data processing industry uses in vying for a share of the $1 billion a year spent by cities and counties on data processing (Danziger, 1977, p. 28).

The experience of local governments with data processing is particularly important, since local governments have had enough experience to work through the initial infatuation and take a close, hard look at the real impact on their organization and its service delivery potential. Because many local government functions are similar across the United States, they have also had limited experience with the more sophisticated and standardized applications—for example, total integrated information systems, simulations, modeling and gaming.

Most local government experience has been with specific information systems such as billing and payroll. Some attempts have been made to develop comprehensive, integrated, urban information systems, but they have not been successful due to a lack of efficiency and exorbitant costs. The push for a total information system may again become popular due to recent advances in computer technology. Distributed systems and microcomputers are now providing the capacity for integrating many of the separate information systems in local governments (Kraemer & King, 1976, p. 18).

Modeling, gaming, and simulations have been applied to many urban problems—for example, land use, public facilities location, vehicle routing, manpower scheduling, water resources management, and citizen participation (Patterson, 1976; Gass & Sisson, 1975; Beltrami, 1977). At present, these advanced computer applications have been more successful at the operational and managerial levels of decision making than at the policy level (Byrd, 1975, p. 249).

Considerations Developed from the Experiences of Local Governments

Preimplementation

Concerns on when to computerize are usually related to personnel, cost, and the political climate. Cost is still the major consideration; but this consideration is changing from whether or not to implement data processing to which type of application will the benefits exceed the costs. Clearly, systems of record keeping and analysis, utility billing, payroll, and tax accounting have justified the costs invested. Kraemer and King (1976) sum up the cost-benefit question as follows:

> Among the technical benefits are increased speed of information processing, greater availability of information, greater consistency of reports, increased capacity to handle large volumes of data, ability to perform repetitive data processing and record-keeping tasks easily, as well as greater operational capabilities for providing new services, monitoring expenditures, investing cash reserves, taxing equitably, and meeting deadlines on state reporting requirements. The obvious costs associated with these technical benefits include the personnel, training, facilities, and equipment required to develop and operate the systems, both in the data processing unit and the user departments. (p. 8)

Cost-benefit considerations are extremely difficult to measure because of the hidden costs associated with development, maintenance, modification, and training, and the difficulty of measuring the dollar benefits such as those associated with a more accurate billing system. Productivity from data processing is likely to result from cost avoidance rather than cost savings or cost displacement (U. of Texas, Note 25).

Although cost benefit is a major concern, it is highly dependent on other significant factors such as the mode of operation and how much of the system will be developed from scratch or transferred from other governments or private firms.

The transfer of a high-cost computer application from one organization to another to save development costs seems a logical idea to reduce overall costs. However, Kraemer (1977, pp. 371-376) neither supporting nor discrediting technology transfers, offers some sobering considerations. They are as follows:

1. The process of developing computer applications offers in-house staff an exceptional opportunity to develop computing capability within the constraints of local skill, time, and money available. In contrast, application transfers may actually prevent learning.

2. Considerable evidence indicates the best candidates for technology transfers are those organizations with a highly developed electronic data processing (EDP) staff. Being sophisticated, these governments can better assess the potential of application before they are implemented by outside experts. In addition, they are capable of undertaking the complexities of their own independent search, evaluation, and transfer.

3. Technology transfers may increase resistance and decrease future use. It is usually an abrupt change that cannot sufficiently involve and educate the user.

4. Cost savings only occur when the automated task is truly general, when the application has been well documented and designed for transfer, when the computer program fits the transferee's current computing capability, and when the application is relatively self-contained.

5. Development savings from technology transfers may be depleted by cost for operations and maintenance. Some applications are expensive to operate because they were not designed with operation and maintenance costs in mind. Others are expensive because the originators issue frequent changes or enhancements that have to be implemented, and still others require new data collection and updating procedures not previously performed.

6. Transfer barriers due to hardware and programming language are lessening, but few systems are designed for transfer due to local institutional and behavioral factors. Adequate documentation is rare.

7. Successful examples of software transfers are rare.

Danziger (1977, pp. 31-34) examines some other cost-related assumptions usually associated with electronic data processing (EDP) systems. His analysis of these assumptions is worth summarizing here.

Assumption. EDP tends to be staff reducing and cost reducing. Staff reductions are an exception rather than the rule. In a government in which patronage exists, there is a reluctance to eliminate the kinds of jobs automation might affect. Civil service protection may also prevent staff reduction. The most common effect for nonclerical workers is a change in the nature of jobs rather than job elimination. Another potential problem is that computer capacity is planned on future needs and after the demands of implementation are over, the excess staff time and computer capacity are used to initiate new luxury projects that are job protecting.

Assumption. EDP turns mountains of data into molehills. Because data are easy to collect and store, information systems tend to stimulate the overaccumulation of data. Usually no criteria exist to separate necessary from desirable from superfluous data. So computers can turn mountains of data into molehills, but they can also turn mountains of data into mountain ranges.

Assumption. EDP provides better information for decision making. Having better information does not assure that it will be used in decision making. Another problem is that people tend not to question computerized information. It is sometimes considered accurate when it is based on tenuous assumptions.

Assumption. EDP increases the supervisor's ability to manage subordinates. The increased ability to control and monitor subordinates can dramatically change how people perform their work. The behavioral and morale problems sometimes associated with this capacity, however, can result in worse rather than better performance by subordinates.

Assumption. Inadequate utilization of EDP is primarily due to user ignorance or resistance. Within the user department, the best predictors of successful implementation and use of a new computer application seem to be (a) the extent to which EDP has generally infiltrated the standard operating procedures of the unit, and (b) either or both the familiarity with EDP or the level of professionalism of the manager of the unit. The most common problem is the unit in charge of EDP. Many local governments, hamstrung by civil service requirements regarding hiring, salary, and promotion, have an inadequate EDP staff which is part of the user problem. User involvement is encouraged in cases in which programmers and analysts are (a) decentralized to user departments and are in the user chain of command, (b) are personnel with actual job experience in the user department, or (c) are programmed by the EDP unit to have a fundamental user orientation.

Other preimplementation concerns developed from local government experience are

1. The acquisition, training, and retention of qualified personnel will be the most demanding and difficult task (U. of Texas, Note 25).
2. Most of those who reflect on EDP in local government are committed to its success. They focus on successful uses, "they confuse potential with performance and they vigorously teach the EDP catechism" (Danziger, 1977, p. 35).
3. If the computer function is to maximize its capabilities and be most effective, it should be under the supervision of top management and not placed within a department (U. of Texas, Note 25).

Implementation

As with business, the behavioral aspects of the implementation process are the most important. The behavioral aspects of local government are especially complex with conflicting interests, changing goals, civil service, and other political considerations. Involvement again seems the key to reducing resistance and assuring use of the system. It is not only important to involve those groups internal to the system, but also groups who are external. A citizens' advisory group of community people knowledgeable in computers can be a needed buffer to the potential problems that inevitably happen. However, one should be careful that experts on this panel do not try to push their pet approach (U. of Texas, Note 25).

Daniel (1976) points out some recommendations to insure in-house user acceptance.

1. Pinpoint immediate strengths and long-range advantages of MIS to employees affected.

2. Prepare a strong orientation program and keep the entire organization informed and current of events.
3. Sincerely support and promote MIS to employees and management. Make sure that MIS objectives are known and not hidden.
4. Attempt to put affected employees at ease about any systems change and maintain personal contact with those elements throughout the period of change.
5. Upward mobility can be associated with employee acceptance of change.
6. Acceptance and adaptability to change should be one of the appraisal elements in every manager's career appraisal. (p. 21)

Another area of concern in implementing any data processing effort is the issue of privacy. This problem is accentuated with computers because of the large quantity of integrated data collected and its easy retrieval. Dial and Goldberg (1975, pp. 1-2) point to the fact that the smaller the scale of data processing activity, the greater the vulnerability of a city to data processing abuse. Studies have indicated that most abuses against government computer centers have occurred in local units of government, collusion has a high frequency of occurrence, and the number of perpetrators is surprisingly large per case. This occurs because of the lack of sophistication of small governments, the multiple roles each person plays in various systems, after-hour opportunities associated with a single shift operation, few formal written procedures, and the general effects of an informal setting. The solution Dial and Goldberg advocate involves implementing ordinances, regulations, standards of ethics, and continual monitoring.

A good summary of the concerns during implementation is presented by Kraemer and King (1976, p. 23). If the following tasks are done poorly, there is little hope for a successful system.

1. Designing the systems to fit properly into local government organizations.

2. Including users in the development of information systems, and seeing to it that they share responsibility for the resultant system.
3. Providing the finances for adequate systems development and operation.
4. Handling organizational and other human impacts that result from the system.
5. Protecting confidentiality and privacy.
6. Evaluating the performance of the information system.

Postimplementation

Given the complexities of competing interests in any local government, it is not surprising that the effects of data processing are diverse and sometimes disputed. Again, research is necessary to determine what effects are more likely than others and in what situations, for as Danziger (1977) notes, "there is evidence that the impacts of EDP upon many local governmant operations are complex and might be, at least in part, negative" (p. 35).

Downs (1967) noted the following power shifts due to the information a computerized information system generates.

Lower and intermediate-level officials will tend to lose power to higher-level officials and politicians.

High-level staff officials will gain power.

Local government legislators will lose power to administrators and operating officials.

The government bureaucracy as a whole will gain power at the expense of the general electorate and nongovernmental groups.

Well-organized and sophisticated groups of all kinds, including some government bureaucrats, will gain power at the expense of less well-organized and less sophisticated groups.

Within local governments, those who actually control automated data systems will gain power at the expense of those who do not.

Technically educated officials within local governments will gain power at the expense of old-style political advisors.

Kraemer and King (1976, p. 9) indicate Down's power shifts do not occur in data processing of routine operational tasks but have proven true in systems which supply information past lower-level managers to top managers, systems that store and process data valuable for political and administrative purposes, and systems that exist for intelligence purposes such as criminal data banks.

The impacts due to having an information system in an organization are more subtle and effect most local governments. They are as follows (Kraemer & King, 1976, p. 10).

1. Executives may lose flexibility in resource allocation due to the requirements of maintaining and improving computerized systems.
2. Executives may find that computerized systems create numerous new issues that demand time and attention.
3. Executives may lose control over portions of their information system due to requirements for participation in state or nationwide systems.
4. Executives may find it difficult to maintain access, oversight, and coordination over data handling that was previously controlled by each department.
5. Executives may face problems due to departmentally shared data files.

These impacts greatly affect the management of the organization and must be dealt with in a way that maximizes both the utility of the technology and the effectiveness of government management.

Some of the more sophisticated computer applications to local government decision making have had impacts that deserve consideration. In a study of the effects of Fiscal

Impact Budgeting Systems on local governments, Dutton and Kraemer (1978) found that the assumptions made and the information generated was too complex for local government decision makers to understand and use. Consequently in many instances, Fiscal Impact Budgeting Systems automated existing biases into the decision making process and increased the influences of departments over elected officials.

Concluding Remarks

We have seen that local governments have learned much from their experiences with data processing. Many of the successes so often promised seem the exception rather than the rule and require knowledge, experience, and hard work by all involved. Even so, it seems that a data processing system is a tool that many local governments cannot afford to be without. Data processing applications have become part of government and their influences are pervading all levels of decision making. As an integral part of government, they have some of the same characteristics. Both are necessary processes we cannot avoid, but must live with and learn to make the most of.

Chapter 9

THE EXPERIENCE IN HUMAN SERVICES

Overview

Government at all levels in the United States spends over $250 billion a year on human services and this amount is likely to increase, especially if defense spending and inflation can be curtailed. In the last few years, state budgets have expanded most rapidly in the area of human services, particularly from Medicaid and public assistance (*Roles for General Purpose Governments*, 1976, p. v). Along with this rapid pace of growth, human service programs have been plagued by management problems and constant turmoil at all levels, including national goal setting. With the disillusionment in the Great Society programs at the end of the 1960s, extensive data-collection efforts were initiated to gain some form of control and accountability over the massive bureaucracy of agencies, grants, and contracts that had developed (Noah, 1978, p. 103).

The computer, which had proven its information-processing and control capabilities at the Department of Defense and at the National Aeronautics and Space Administration, became an integral part of the data-collection effort, but due to costs could only be introduced at the management level in federal, state, and large urban agencies. But while information systems became an integral part of many federal and state human service systems, the fragmentation and diversity of services at the community level prevented all but experimental efforts. Thus local agency personnel have had contact with only large information systems and presently are not familiar with smaller community or agency systems. Several national surveys on mental health information systems exist (see Franklin, Note 6; Schnibbe & Praschil, Note 17; Hedlund, Vieweg, Cho, Evensen, Hickman, Holland, Vogt, Wolf, & Wood, Note 9).

At the local agency level, costs have been a prohibitive factor. A 1977 United Way of America study (Note 24, p. i) found widespread use of computers in the budgeting process of local United Ways, but only recent efforts in developing comprehensive systems that integrate data for planning, budgeting, information and referral, and volunteer skills into a single reporting structure. A check with the national offices of several other human services revealed little or no information system activities. For example, Family Service of America, the national association for one of the most common nonfederal human service agencies, estimated that only 10% of its members had any computer processing activity, and most purchased computer time for budgeting purposes only (McCurdy, Note 10). With the cost of computers dropping, however, computerized information systems that can be transferred throughout a variety of similar agencies are beginning to be developed.

Because the experience of human service agencies has not been as extensive as that of business and local government, the literature contains less information to guide the practitioner. Boyd, Hylton, and Price (1978), in a review of nine social work journals between 1970 and 1976, found 31 articles on the use of a computer application in the human services. They concluded,

It would appear that computers in social welfare settings have been used almost exclusively for clerical work, record keeping, and accounting. . . . The computer was occasionally used to assist in program planning and in making budetary decisions. Generally, however, these uses were only secondary and the system had, in fact, been designated for more routine administrative tasks. The use of the computer as a potential tool to aid the direct-service worker was unrecognized in the professional literature. Also ignored was the need to incorporate computer training in the education of professional social workers. (p. 370)

Government documents are a much richer source of information. Several guidebooks for community mental health centers are extremely helpful (Cooper, 1973; Chapman, 1976; Dreyer, Bellerby & Koroloff, 1979; Paton & D'Huyvetter, 1980). Cooper focuses on data and accounting systems, whereas Chapman focuses on operational systems such as intake, service delivery, and evaluation. Dreyer, Bellerby & Koroloff have developed several self-help workbooks on information system improvement, while Paton and D'Huyvetter present a conceptual as well as practice guide on community mental health center information systems.

A summary of some of the considerations and problems associated with the preimplementation, implementation, and postimplementation phase of computerized information systems follows. Because the experience has not been vast, implementation considerations and especially postimplementation considerations are few and point to the urgent need for further research. A further limitation is that most of the considerations mentioned were developed from state, county, or large metropolitan efforts and may not apply to small agency efforts or to distributed systems.

Considerations Developed from the Experiences of Human Services

Preimplementation

In planning any system the first consideration is locating a secure funding source that will support the system development effort from start to evaluation and modification. Multiple funding is superior to a single unguaranteed source. A system effort that is constantly seeking continuation funds loses the strength and impetus it needs to secure the commitment and energy from those involved.

Another obvious major consideration is the cost-benefit analysis. In large part, the cost-benefit analysis depends on the level of sophistication desired, the rate of implementation, and the reliability required. A few of the most salient cost benefit considerations that have not been discussed previously are listed below.

1. The cost and benefit of any particular system must be examined in relation to the overall agency goal of providing services to the community (Laska & Bank, 1975, p. 57). "Most agencies that do not have definitive descriptions of their current activities would be shocked to discover just where their resources are going" (Chapman, 1976, p. 9).

2. The voluntary social welfare sector has evidenced much misunderstanding and indecisiveness in regard to what is expected of its information systems. "The social welfare field tends to be reactive rather than proactive but has neither designed systems to accommodate this fact nor changed the style of decision making, planning, and administration so that management information systems can be of greater utility" (Polivy & Salvatore, 1976, p. 68).

3. The more an agency must rely on the information system for daily operational functions, the higher the reliability required and the higher the cost.

4. Hardware maintenance costs are minor when compared to the cost of maintaining the software (Crawford, Morgan & Gianturco, 1974, p. 345).

5. A key reality about information systems is that they often increase paperwork and staff, or at least the staff size remains constant. The positive aspect is

that the system enables the staff to do a better job and serve people in a more effective manner (Bowers & Bowers, 1977, p. 48).

6. Although the total cost for an agency may increase due to the increased demand revealed by an information system, the cost of services rendered per client may decrease (Chapman, 1976, pp. 9 & 39).

7. A billing system integrated with the agency information system can generate additional sources of funds from clients and third-party payers, as well as save in personnel costs.

8. Benefits will not automatically be derived from implementing a management information system, but hinges on management's ability to use the system. A management information system allows research and evaluation capacity that would probably not be undertaken manually. A management information system enables the agency to improve the overall quality of care delivered to its clients (Paton & D'Huyvetter, 1980, pp. 227-228).

The Paton and D'Huyvetter guide contains a chapter on how to obtain a rough measure of the costs and benefits associated with an agency management information system. Although their guide is based on their experience in community mental health centers, it probably has considerable value for similar human service agencies, for example, family service agencies.

Another preimplementation consideration is the rate of implementation. The best procedure is considered an incremental approach, but with the concept of building a total system in mind (Percy, 1977, p. 205; Cooper, 1973, p. 3). For as Mittenthal (1976) points out,

Information systems are not total human service systems. Moreover, they are a tool, not an answer. The danger is that designed in a vacuum, an information system may not even be an effective tool, or at least its cost may outweigh its benefit. An information system or data unit should be designed in the context of an overall system.... Yet, too often, information systems are bought without a clear specification of their purpose, or proper understanding of their relationship to other system components (p. 146).

The system should be modular, flexible, and as simple as possible to accommodate the changes that will inevitably occur due to factors outside the organization such as new federal reporting requirements or new directions that become obvious from the initial development effort (Bowers & Bowers, 1977, pp. 44-45). It should also be based on extensive planning, reflect the relationship of organizational components, be oriented toward management and staff, be open to expansion, be discriminating in the data it collects and disseminates, and rely on the common data flows within the agency (Paton & D'Huyvetter, 1980, pp. 79-81).

Other notes of caution during the preimplementation phase follow.

1. Most successful system development efforts can be traced back to a key decision maker or leader. Such key persons must have a thorough understanding of the politics of the situation as well as knowledge of both agency programs and systems. They must also be able to compromise and must be respected and accepted by the main players in the development environment (Bowers & Bowers, 1977, p. 39).

2. Perhaps the most apparent weakness in human service information systems is the absence of proper documentation or any documentation at all. Inadequate documentation makes it difficult for new employees to make a smooth transition when they take over information systems responsibilities. In addition, it has frustrated potential system transfer

efforts to other localities. Documentation is both a boring exercise to most system designers and a hard item to justify as cost beneficial to the developing organization. Generally it is not required by decision makers, because they underestimate its value (Bowers & Bowers, 1977, p. 49).

3. It is wise to plan for an early payoff or visible demonstration of results.

4. "Test, test, and then test again. The tendency to rush into implementation, including the printing of forms, prior to a good 'ironing out' of the system, has too often proven to be a costly mistake" (Bowers & Bowers, 1976, p. 96).

Paton and D'Huyvetter (1980, Ch. 7) discuss an organization's preparedness for implementing a management information system. Figure 9-1 presents the framework that is useful in identifying the important variables of preparedness.

Implementation

Perhaps the most important consideration during implementation is the involvement of all potential users in all parts and phases of the development, particularly the design phase. Although this involvement is time consuming and frustrating, it is almost mandatory for long-range success.

One method to ensure user involvement is to provide adequate resources for training and educating potential users, so they have the ability to become meaningfully involved. To have quality system output, users must learn how to input accurately into the system. Another method is to make one of the uses of the data collected that of determining productivity and performance in an incentive system. Professionals have far less resistance to collecting data about their work if their remuneration depends on it (Wilder & Miller, 1973, p. 130).

Figure 9-1.   Framework for assessing a Community Mental Health Center's preparedness for MIS

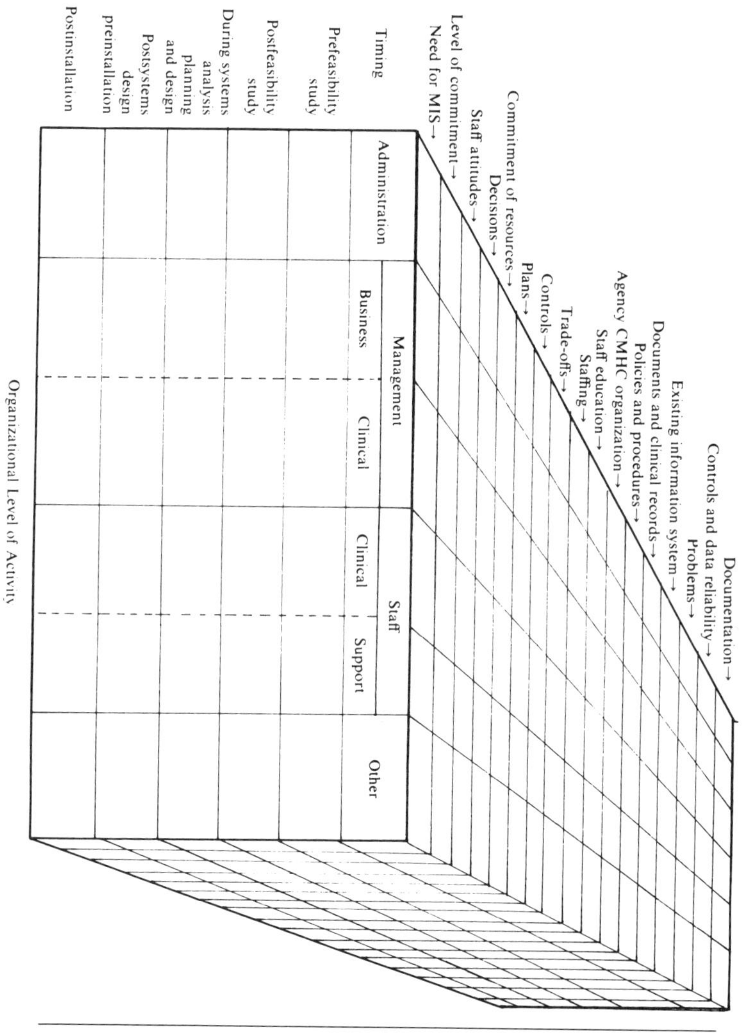

Note. From *Automated Management Information Systems for Mental Health Agencies: A Planning and Acquisition Guide* by J. Paton and P. D'huyvetter, U.S. Department of Health and Human Services, NIMH Mental Health Service System Reports (Series FN No 1), 1980, p. 56.

One common source of problems during the implementation effort is that too much authority is given or taken by the systems people. Top management must involve themselves in the development effort and continue to set policy rather than let the computer system or the design personnel evolve policy. The implementation of new organizational systems calls for many major decisions and creates many power vacuums. Systems people are sometimes all too ready to accept or take authority. They do not necessarily have the same goals as agency people and have a tendency to do the most that is technically possible rather than that which is usable and affordable (Bowers & Bowers, 1976, p. 96). Chapman (1976, p. 11) recommends that the development effort be directly responsible to top management rather than report through several organization layers. Compounding the problem is the fact that people in the human services and the computer programmers are clearly from two different worlds. They even speak in two mutually incomprehensible languages (Quinn, 1976, p. 171).

Finally, the issue of confidentiality and privacy is sure to emerge. It should be considered in its proper context, however, for as Chapman (1976, p. 9) notes, the confidentiality of client data in an information system is only a small part of the policy reorientation precipitated by recent court and legislative action. Present in-house computerized information systems can be made just as secure as paper-and-pencil file systems, as Vondracek, Urban, and Parsonage (1974) indicate:

> The question to be asked is whether the use of computers forces on the professional a compromise regarding his standards for confidentiality. The answer is a resounding no. Strict security measures for the collecting, processing, and recording of all confidential data can and must be established when the system is initially designed. Typically, this is accomplished by assigning computer access codes to each qualified user of the computer system. . . . Furthermore, any specified user with a

given access code may be allowed to receive only certain types of information about certain cases in the system. (pp. 277-278)

Two notes of warning during the implementation process deserve mentioning.

First, the design team should avoid unofficial conflict resolution or organizational repair on the problems they uncover. These problems should be handled by traditional hierarchial methods so as not to focus agency tension on the team and jeopardize its function (Chapman, 1976, p.12).

Second, staff members inevitably see the introduction of a system as a personal threat. Thus every effort, every report, and every change must be designed to deemphasize the individual and focus on programs (Fein, 1975, p. 24).

Postimplementation

Information management applications have a profound effect on any organization, but especially human service agencies as they are usually unsystematic in their operation, and the logic and precision required by a sophisticated data base means radical changes. This change and the precise documentation create stress as well as accentuate present problems, as Chapman (1976) points out, "An MIS is a powerful tool in the sense that it brings problems out into the open. Not all organizations are prepared to deal with stark reality" (p. 9).

Trust seems to become a very important variable in how an organization handles this "stark reality." Staff must trust peer review and management review of their performance. This is particularly true of a total agency information system that tracks staff successes and failures as well as detailed time and effort reports. If personnel feel that any of the information will be used against them, they will resist and possibly sabotage the system (Paton, Note 15). Personnel should be forewarned that information systems will bring changes, because when changes occur, they tend to occur from the top down, not the bottom up (Chapman, 1976, p. 11). It also seems to be important that clinicians see that computerized information systems will not change their basic role—that is, evaluating, observing, and treating clients—rather, it will change the manner in which they perform their role (Crawford et al., 1974, p. 342).

Concluding Remarks

The previous discussion points out that information management can be a beneficial and worthwhile venture in the human services, but a strong agency and staff are needed to handle the stress and the change that any application creates. Research is needed to answer basic questions; for example, what are the effects of an information management application on morale, the power structure, the agency structure, and so on? We know little. The literature points more to the pains and mistakes than to the effects and benefits. Clearly, at this point it seems most agencies should consider a major information management effort as a radical restructuring of their present way of functioning and proceed with caution: for although the end result is desirable, the experience is not.

Information Management in Two Human Services Areas

Public Assistance

Computerized information management activities are occurring at a rapid pace in public assistance agencies. The impetus seems to stem from the income maintenance rather than the social service function of the agencies. The demand for accountability and productivity stem primarily from the large amount of taxpayers' money spent each year in the more controversial programs of the welfare system. Although the demand for computerization of management data is coming from the top down, the demand for computerization of case management data is coming from the workers at the line level (Nakamoto, Note 12), (Neilson, Note 14).

Organizations such as the American Public Welfare Association (APWA) are another significant force, having taken an active lead in joining with the government to assure that the management needs of agencies are met. For example, the APWA on contract with the Department of Health, Education and Welfare conducted three regional conferences in the spring of 1978 for state data processing personnel (Shute, Note 20). The conferences allowed the federal government to determine at what stage of development each state was, and allowed state data processing personnel to share ideas, problems, solutions, and the latest technology. Currently a vast difference exists between states in information management application. States that have sophisticated systems in income maintenance may be totally lacking in automation of their social services and vice versa. Automation seems to be dependent on a state's willingness and ability to experiment and the federal government's willingness to help pay the bill.

Present and Potential Information Management Applications.   Information systems have primarily been a management tool, especially in the income maintenance areas such as Medicare and Medicaid. Besides statistical reporting and accounting, which are automated in almost all states, certain states such as Maine and South Dakota are also using the computer to determine client eligibility for financial and social services.

The potential exists for adding additional applications to computerized eligibility determination. Coupled with a determination printout, there could be an information and referral sheet of eligible vendors and an authorization form. Specialized applications could perform additional functions such as determining the level of nursing-home care (Lopez-Toledo, 1976). In income maintenance as well as in social services, management could use the computer as a personnel tool. The computer can easily assign, track, and evaluate workers and provide programmed education and training on many of the basic welfare tasks and regulations. Besides collecting, tabulating, and printing reports for management, a computerized data base is an extremely useful research tool. Due to the computer's ability to scan rapidly large volumes of data, it can sift through client records to produce a profile of those clients on whose record errors are known to have been made, or those clients who in the past were high-risk cases or required special attention, or even those convicted of fraud. With these profiles in the computer's memory, the computer could notify the intake worker at the time of eligibility determination of the possibility of a special situation. The intake worker could then determine whether this special situation exists and act accordingly (Nakamoto, Note 12). With intake information input directly into the data base via remote terminal, these profile checks could be run automatically. If a problem profile is identified, additional questions could be instantaneously provided the worker to allow for more data collection in the problem area.

For the worker, computerized information and referral aides and automated client data are becoming common. Much less common are automated case management systems that contain data and information on such variables as the initial level of need or client functioning, the plan of action to correct the problem or satisfy the need, the units of service delivered by agency and by cost, and the progress made according to the initial plan. Efficiency and effectiveness measures could also be an integral part of the automated case management records.

Problems Associated with Computer Uses in Public Assistance Agencies. Many of the problems encountered in public assistance agencies are similar to those in other agencies. Costs are still a significant factor, although distributed systems and the minicomputer are beginning to offer tremendous flexibility at reasonable costs (Shute, Note 20; Teal, Note 23).

Good programming and design personnel are scarce; at present no special background seems to dominate this new profession. The ability to understand both information management and the value nuances of an organization as complex as a public assistance agency makes good program and design personnel a rarity (Racine, Note 16). No profession seems to be training this type of personnel.

Ignorance and fear of automation from the top levels of HHS on down to the agency casework level are problems. The result is that computerized data and information are not maximally used in making decisions, thus minimizing the benefits derived from the large costs invested. Sabotage by management can also become a problem. The ability of an information system to document management deficiencies has created situations in which, to save itself, management has labeled the system as a costly failure and quickly removed it.

Part of the constraints on an automated case management system are inherent in the vendor system of services. Although the automation of income maintenance programs is an in-house function, automation of client information involves the whole community. Public assistance agencies have no authority or funds to encourage other agencies to become part of a case management information system. As a result, many communities have, at best, only a loosely coordinated group of individual services rather than a tightly coordinated or integrated network of services. Congress also refuses to take an integrated approach to service delivery, preferring to modify existing categorical programs rather than develop integrated systems. The politics, power, and jurisdiction disputes attached to each categorical program seem likely to continue.

Perhaps the most serious problem in public assistance agencies is that of constant change at the top levels of decision making. A rational, planned system is impossible when the goals of the system change due to new administrations, new legislation, new bureaucratic appointments, and new initiatives. Information management is dependent on stable goals and objectives and becomes difficult with the haphazard "political football" approach taken toward welfare in our democratic society. Another related problem is that research is considered a very low priority by the federal government. Whereas private industry spends 3% to 20% of their budget on research, some areas of the federal government, such as Medicare and Medicaid, have little or nothing designated in their budgets for research (Nakamoto, Note 12).

Future Applications. What applications are seen for the next 10 years in public assistance agencies? The best educated guesses indicate that income maintenance may be a credit card operation with electronic fund transfers. Social service employees, with beepers strapped to their belts, will have constant communication with their agency's computer which schedules, furnishes route plans, and tracks their progress. Managers can count on computer simulations of their services that use economic and social indicators (such as their projected budget, the local unemployment rate, local economic data, and census data) to predict what decisions should be made to maximize their limited resources; HHS is already beginning work on basic simulations for public assistance agencies (Greenberg, Note 7). These changes will rarely be found in one place. Different states will experiment with different systems and only when success is achieved on a cost-effectiveness basis will the development spread across the United States.

Occurring alongside these more sophisticated applications will be the move toward what Nolan termed in Chapter

7 as the third and fourth stages of data processing; that is, agency-wide data bases will be developed, and data management will be recognized as a crucial organizational function and placed in a separate department headed by an information services executive who is an integral part of top management. All these changes will be gradual and constant over the next 5 to 15 years. Overall they will add up to an impressive system change with information management as a basic component of decision making in the service delivery system.

An Illustration: The Child Welfare Information Services of New York

An example of a progressive information management application is the Child Welfare Information Services (CWIS), Inc., of New York. (The following discussion is based on CWIS, Note 4.)

Child Welfare Information Services (CWIS) is a nonprofit, information services bureau controlled by a 24-member board composed of representatives of eight public agencies, eight voluntary agencies, four state agencies, and representatives from four private child interest groups. Its purpose is to provide an accountability and planning mechanism and an integrated community data base for research and evaluation. It began in 1972 with a 13-person staff and a budget of $411,000. It has since been expanded statewide under legislative order and presently has approximately 59 staff and a $1,865,000 budget.

The CWIS's functions could be classified in two basic areas, data collection management and retrieval, and user support. The CWIS's major function is to develop and maintain a community data base on child welfare services in New York. It automates the information generated on the child and the family in the intake interview and updates the data whenever significant changes occur in client status. The data that agencies provide are automatically processed through approximately 200 validity checks to flag errors such as contradictory data—for example, 45-year old children. Errors are returned to the caseworker for correction. The data base is the source of automated billing and the generation of over 200 reports to caseworkers, supervisors, executives, and for the system as a whole. These reports include such things as lists, counts, ticklers or reminders, mandated forms, special studies, and a microfiche of the computer file on each client. Types of data produced for agencies are listings of the services offered by agencies or districts, detailed statistics by agency and district, and overall agency and district ratings on 31 performance indicators. Privacy is protected in all reports based on a written agreement between CWIS and the participating agency. Reports are safeguarded by various levels of confidentiality, such as system-wide nonidentifiable data, agency-identifiable data, client-identifiable data, and restricted data available only to the submitting agency.

The second major service of CWIS is user support. It has a large agency relations department that handles all user communications, issues, and procedures; provides training; handles problems and special reports; and interprets data and reports for the user. The importance of the agency relations functions can be seen by its workload, which includes answering approximately 3,000 user calls per month and training over 100 persons per month.

The major impact of CWIS is in the development of a data base for the community child welfare delivery system, and the development of a common language for that system. The CWIS data allow for the development of system-wide monitoring and control standards and mechanisms that can be used to move the system in the direction of goal achievement. Once system goals are defined, performance criteria can be developed to insure that agencies can monitor their progress towards achieving these goals. For example, CWIS statistics indicate that 60% of the 28,000 children in the system have not seen their parents in the last 6 months. This indicates that either the system is failing by not encouraging family ties, or that the system is heavily loaded with abandoned children. Using visits with parents as a performance indicator could help correct this situation. Another possible performance indicator is revealed by the CWIS data that show children remaining in the child care system for an average of 5.1 years. This data point out that the system may simply be warehousing many children rather than making permanent plans for them. Clearly CWIS points to the potential of a community data base in documenting what the existing system is doing and in monitoring efforts to change the system to improve services to clients.

One major benefit of CWIS is that it saves $10 for each dollar it spends. Its major savings, over $5 million a year in interest charges, are due to the speedup of claims and billings. The 10:1 ratio probably does not include the savings due to the system providing more efficient permanent placements, thus placing state-financed foster children into non-subsidized or minimally subsidized adoptive homes. It also does not reflect the savings that may occur over the next 5 to 20 years due to the increased mental status of children who are placed rather than warehoused. Other major savings occur in the area of program evaluation and special studies. Studies and evaluations that previously took months to complete are now simple with CWIS's computerized data base.

Other effects of CWIS include the ability to provide timely information on lawsuits against the child welfare system and the ability to determine quickly the impact of proposed legislative action—for example, budget cutbacks, reimbursement formulas, and so on—on specific services to children and on the total system performance. Probably the most significant potential impact is in the area of social policy and social legislations. The CWIS data have major implications for state and national child welfare goals and priorities: for only when we can document what we are doing can we specify the direction in which we should be moving.

Community Mental Health

Community mental health centers, with their state and federal ties to funds, are probably the most advanced locally controlled, personal social service agency in the use of computerized application. Due to their local control, however, each center is unique and uses the computer in its own way depending on factors such as computer availability, state emphasis, agency sophistication with data, and management interest. The past decade has seen the community mental health center become a prime deliverer of mental health, mental retardation and other personal social services in communities across the United States. With the present emphasis on deinstitutionalization and the provision of the least restrictive services to clients, community mental health centers are continuing to develop an array of preventive, semiinstitutional, and community services for a wide spectrum of community residents.

Although the burden for providing services has grown, the ability of community mental health centers to generate adequate operating funds is becoming increasingly difficult. Legislatures and other funding sources are asking for hard documentation that their limited dollars are being wisely spent. For example, Public Law 94-63, Title III, required community mental health centers to establish an effective procedure for developing, compiling, evaluating, and reporting statistics and other information relating to the cost of the center's operation and the patterns of utilization of its services. Additionally, it requires centers to establish a program evaluation capacity (Percy, 1977, p. 204).

Fulfilling reporting requirements and documenting results require data and lots of it. Just providing state and federal program data, such as professional standards review organization (PSRO) and Title XX, requires a substantial data collection effort by any community mental health center. With additional program evaluation data collection and manipulation mandated, it is no wonder that agencies are looking for solutions to their data problems. As Slavin (1978) notes, "Pressure for accountability and auditing requirements by funding agencies, legislatures, and by governmental bodies purchasing services may suggest no alternative but to install a competent system" (p. 479).

Attempts to establish total agency information systems in the last decade have to date not had the success everyone has hoped for:

> Designing an information processing system to serve all agency information processing needs would be a very arduous task. Attempts to do so have proved to be very expensive and time consuming, and there has not been complete user satisfaction with the operation of these multipurpose systems. (Chapman, 1976, p. 5)

A major problem preventing community mental health centers from computerizing other than accounting and client data systems has been obtaining financial support; and a second basic problem has been obtaining the strong backing needed from all concerned not only to see that the system is implemented, but also to see it through the several years needed to complete an adequate trial period (Crawford et al., 1974, p. 346).

Most information management applications in community mental health centers have been with large and costly state or multiagency computer systems, or on time-sharing arrangements that are cumbersome to use and aggravate problems of confidentiality and turn-around time. With computer hardware becoming less expensive, however, it is becoming financially feasible for a community mental health center to buy an in-house minicomputer rather than pay for data processing services. An in-house computer solves many problems, such as confidentiality and turn-around time, and allows maximum flexibility in developing a total agency information system.

Many people see present experiments with minicomputers and distributed systems as a determining factor on what will happen next. Developing a reliable in-house computer-based agency information system that is cost efficient and capable of being used by community mental health centers across the United States is considered an adequate 5- to 10-year goal. It seems only a matter of time before mental health centers, like business and local government, accept some form of in-house computer-based information system as an aid they cannot do without. The major deterrents at present are cost, design expertise, and experience that can help iron out the problems associated with any new effort.

Although computer applications to managerial decisions have taken the form of management information systems, computer applications to therapy or the therapist-client interaction have taken a different focus. Because it is extremely difficult to quantify and standardize therapeutic goals and objectives and data related to decision making at the therapy level, data bases and information systems to address therapy decisions have not been developed. Rather than developing computerized data bases at the therapy level, the focus has been on using computers to (a) perform routine tasks associated with the client-therapist interaction—for example, analyze test results and manipulate substantial amounts of coded information; (b) interact with the client in performing a few of the more routine therapeutic functions—for example, perform intake interviews and administration of tests; and (c) simulate or model client behavior or client problematic situations—for example, predict suicide and client role playing. These applications require a limited data base and little or no definition of the therapy process.

The point to be made is that because community mental health centers, unlike business or government, require complex decision making at both the strategic and operational levels, present information systems have primarily been designed around the routine data needs of mid-level managers. Decision support systems that address the more nonprogrammable decisions at the therapeutic and top decision-making levels are not being developed in centers to aid the therapist, because the sophisticated data bases on which a decision support system operates are extremely difficult to develop. Consequently, nondata base computer applications will continue to be developed, refined, and added to the agency computer which will be oriented around the needs of middle management. Although the nondata base applications are exciting, they do not have the overall potential of a decision support system at the therapeutic level. (For an example of how a decision support system could be developed at the therapeutic level, see the section on decision support systems in Chap. 2.)

Since nondata-based applications will continue to comprise a form of computer-based applications in community mental health centers, they will be reviewed below. Most are experimental in nature and not funded on a continuing basis, but they point to the potential that an in-house computer has for a community mental health center. (For an extensive bibliography on the more therapeutic uses of computers, see Hedlund et al., Note 9).

Automated Interview.   A computer can aid in gathering routine information from the client and arranging that information in a meaningful format. The computer can easily move from a positive answer on a general question to appropriate subroutines that gather more details; checking answers with previous responses could trigger new subroutines to check out perspective problem areas. Even severely disturbed patients are able to operate a computer terminal and state their problems in meaningful terms (Alexander, 1978, p. 59).

The computer-client interface is still a major problem, as well as the ability to gather detailed data, emotional cues, and so on. The computer interview has been acceptable to clients with one-half preferring to be interviewed by a computer rather than by a doctor (Coddington & King, 1972; Reich, Robins, Woodruff, Taibleson, Rich, & Cunningham, 1975; Lucas, 1977; Slack & Slack, 1977). One way to make the computer-assisted interview more acceptable to clinicians is to reduce their paperwork load by using patients and others important to them as sources of client information (Meldman, Harris, Pellicore, & Johnson, 1977). Studies show that clients' self-reports have fared well when compared with other points of view presented by observers, diagnosticians, and others meaningful to the client (Klein, Greist, & Van Cura, 1975, p. 841).

Administration and Interpretation of Tests. Perhaps the most successful clinical use of the computer is that of administering psychological tests. The time savings are usually large and the computer has the advantage of administering the tests in a standard format. Experiments indicate that automated testing is a valuable clinical aid and is quicker, less costly, and more accurate than examination by clinicians (Shuman, 1976; Williams, 1977).

Automated Diagnosis. A logical extension of the computer's interview capacity is the computer diagnosis. The computer's ability to analyze rapidly large quantities of data results in it being an excellent diagnostic tool. One of the problems in determining the accuracy of the computerized clinical diagnosis is that there is sometimes less than unanimous agreement between experienced clinicians on a client's diagnosis. Until the criteria for successful diagnosis are developed, we cannot test the computer's accuracy, only its agreement or disagreement with a group of experts who disagree among themselves. Rather than actual diagnosis, the computer's primary use, however, is more likely to be as a clinician's aid that can point out the problem areas highly associated with the pattern of symptoms exhibited by the client. Initial experiments in this area are promising (Spitzer & Endicott, 1974; Williams, Johnson, & Bliss, 1975; Bailine, Katzoff, & Rau, 1977). Also, given the availability of sufficient storage, the computer could furnish abstracts of the most recent research on the problem areas or diagnostic categories identified.

Therapy. Not surprisingly, the most effective uses of the computer in therapy involve the repetitive and systematic areas of behavior therapy—for example, relaxation, suggestion, and desensitization. Results in this area are comparable to those of experienced clinicians (Thomas, Walter, & O'Flaherty, 1974). The computer is also good at forecasting future client behavior; for example, computers have proven significantly more accurate in predicting suicide attempts than experienced clinicians (Klein et al., 1975, p. 841). Gaming and simulations offer promise in desensitization; for example, a client can role play with an automated simulation model to provide experience in reacting to actual situations (Cassell, 1975). Group therapy is also seen as an area where the computer can provide valuable assistance (Stone & Kristjanson, 1975).

Another valuable aid the computer can easily perform is recommending and monitoring medications (Maronde, 1978). The average psychiatrist could be relieved of an enormous amount of work since the computer could present an up-to-date list of different medications the client is taking or has taken in the past. A list of potential side effects and special precautions based on the client's history and research on the medication could also be produced for the clinician and the client.

Computerized Devices. More related to the developmentally disabled than the mentally ill, computers are seen as offering valuable control and flexibility to devices designed to help the blind see, the amputee walk, and so on (Robinson, 1973). Small computer chips can also be part of brain implantations, which although controversial, can relieve pain and control depression, seizures, and other forms of mental illness.

Education and Training. The areas of education and training offer a vast array of computer uses. Computer games can be fun as well as educational. Algorithms to model the responses given by clients with disorders such as paranoia have been successfully computerized and can easily be used to provide continuing education to therapists (Colby, 1976). The computer combined with video tape has been used for medical education, thus combining the more personalized visual and spoken medium with the memory and manipulation capacity of the computer (Schwartz, Note 18). The future ability of the household TV to become a two-way communication device offers tremendous possibilities for community education about such problems as fear, anxiety, and alcoholism.

Problems. The problem in all the previous clinical applications revolves around the ability to demonstrate that the computer can successfully and reliably perform routine tasks and free the therapist for more problematic and complex clients. Theoretically the computer is less costly, but again the research has not been conducted on a long-term basis to demonstrate the actual cost-benefit over time.

Another major problem area is the computer-client interface. Push the button—yes or no responses are simple, but limited. As some of the more sophisticated techniques are introduced, such as multiple choice and typewriter or symbol keyboards, the number of clients who can interact with the computer are reduced and the processing becomes increasingly complex. Nonmechanical methods, such as the galvanic skin response and voice recognition devices have promise, but require more development (Elwood, Note 5).

Another problem is not having a clinical computer language.

> Just as banks and business found computers more trouble than they were worth until a standard programming language (CO-BOL) became available, psychiatric computer applications have been very difficult and expensive to develop, modify, and disseminate because they have generally been written in languages ill suited to psychiatric applications and run on machines much larger and more expensive than required ... The Bureau of Health Services Research is currently supporting a 3-year standardization of different dialects of MUMPS-MIIS, a high-level computer language specifically developed for clinical use at Massachusetts General Hospital. (Klein et al, 1975, p. 839)

In essence, for a computer to perform the more therapeutic type of tasks, three major components will have to be perfected.

> (1) Computer recognition of the patient's natural language; (2) a conceptual base, embracing both a therapeutic regimen and a profile of the individual patient; and (3) computer responses, expressed in natural-language formats. Each part has its own constellation of difficulties. (Alexander, 1978, p. 54)

This review has by no means exhausted the possibilities of computer use in clinical situations. One has only to play the variety of computer games available on most university computers—for example, Star Trek, Doctor—to become aware of how people can creatively and meaningfully interact with a computer. The popularity of these games also indicates that computer applications can be widely accepted as entertaining as well as educational. If community mental health centers begin to develop in-house computer capacity, research on these clinical nondata base applications of the computer will take a leap forward, and a market for successful applications will be available.

An Illustration: CHARTS of Texas

One of the most advanced Mental Health Center systems to date is the Community Health Automated Record and Treatment System (CHARTS) which was developed in the community mental health centers in Waco and Temple, Texas. (The following discussion is based on CHARTS, Note 3, and a visit to the Waco Center.) Jack Franklin, Chief of Program Analysis and Statistical Research for the Texas Department of Mental Health and Mental Retardation, carried his experience in setting up the state social service information system in North Carolina a step further in setting up the Waco and Temple experiments. In January, 1978, both agencies began operation of an on-line total agency information system designed to manage the information surrounding the therapist. The therapist is the logical focus of a community mental health center information system, because service delivery is the primary mission of a center and those who deliver services are the largest number of potential information system users. To manage the information surrounding the therapeutic process, three major subsystems were developed: (a) a service delivery subsystem, (b) a fund-accounting subsystem, and (c) a clinical records subsystem. These three systems form the basis of decision making and program evaluation at the Waco and Temple community mental health centers.

What ties the three subsystems together is a problem-oriented record approach to client record keeping and a global level of functioning scale (see Fig. 1-3). A problem-oriented record is a type of clinical record that organizes information to identify specific problems the client is experiencing and to facilitate and document the management of these problems. To quote the agency:

> The CHART system is structured to implement a holistic viewpoint of the client through a listing of all problems interfering with the client's independent functioning in his

environment. Careful attention is given to (1) the identification of specific, documentable, objective problems through careful assessment of the client; (2) the selection of appropriate treatment goals; (3) the implementation of problem-specific intervention; and (4) the documentation of efforts to determine if desired results are achieved. (p. 1)

The CHART system is also designed to meet the extended reporting needs of the center including those required by external funding sources and regulatory agencies. Security and privacy are protected by a password requirement, an authorization-level requirement, a matching of report unit to the user's unit, and an archives system for storing files and deleted information.

One of the major features of the system is that it will help therapists manage the information they presently use as well as the new data and information they generate. It is estimated that the system will free therapists to do more counseling by reducing their paperwork by two-thirds. If the system succeeds in this task alone, it will probably be hailed as a success and become a prototype for future efforts.

The cost of the computer hardware was approximately $70,000 to the center. The state is helping pay for the software research and development effort which is being done by Neoterics, Inc., a private software firm. The project is an ambitious attempt, for it stretches the state of the art by trying to develop an integrated information system for several major and basic agency subsystems on a cost-efficient basis for a small agency. It is being watched closely by the National Institute of Mental Health and has already drawn interest from all over the United States. Similar systems are being marketed by CMHC, Inc., of Columbus, Ohio, Systems Technology, Inc., of Atlanta, Georgia, and others.

The most surprising change in the new systems being developed is not in the basic design or performance, but in the reduction of cost; CMHC, Inc. estimates that its basic hardware-software system can be purchased for an average sized mental health center for approximately $50,000 total cost. Cost reduction is in some part due to more efficient design which allows this system to operate on a smaller computer. Major cost reductions, however, are due to rapidly declining computer hardware costs and lower software development costs. It seems that for any system to stay competitive, it will have to be redesigned every 2 to 5 years to fit the newest low-cost computer. The only other alternative is to develop software that is machine independent, an extremely difficult task to perform at this point.

A SYNTHESIS OF GUIDELINES, LIMITATIONS, AND PROBLEM AREAS

Since computerized information management has been with us since the 1950s, a considerable list of "do's and don'ts" has been developed. Many are based on one-time experiences or are limited to a specific type of application. Others, however, seem to occur no matter what the application. Part IV pulls together and elaborates on the guidelines, limitations, and problems from the different theories and organizational experiences discussed in Parts II and III.

As with any pulling together, the conclusions become more powerful because they seem to be mentioned time and time again. At the same time, the advice beccomes more and more general and less specific to any particular situation. Therefore Part IV is to be used not as a cookbook to be followed verbatim, but as a listing of advice that should be considered seriously and accepted or rejected. The essential function of Part IV is the expansion of the thinking process and the bringing of questions out into the open. It is by asking about a specific guideline or problem, or if this limitation or problem applies in our situation, that an agency will give information management the serious consideration it deserves.

Chapter 10

GUIDELINES

Introduction

Many of the guidelines presented here may seem like common sense. The same can be said for much that has been written about management in general; yet, rather than hiring managers based on whether they have good common sense, we hire based on education and experience. For, too many times, common sense does not possess the hindsight and foresight of the more formal approaches to knowledge.

As the term implies these "guidelines" are guides, or statements to help us find our way. They have their limitations, for they apply in general, but specific cases may be exceptions. The guidelines do not include information on whether they are more relevant for a particular type of information management application, whether they apply equally to any level or phase of information management activity, or whether they apply equally to large and small organizations of all types. Therefore the discretion and judgment of the reader is paramount in applying them.

Guidelines

Guideline 1

Planning is required.

As with any of the basic organizational resources—money, people, and facilities—planning is required to insure that future changes in information are in the desired direction and that the end result is the total information management environment that is desired. As Alter and Ginzberg (1978) stress, "The likelihood of successful implementation is positively related to the degree of certainty with which the implementation can be planned" (p. 25).

Four types of plans are necessary:

1. A long-range plan to show the direction in which the organization is headed in information management.
2. An implementation plan for any specific application.
3. An organization adjustment plan.
4. A people adjustment plan.

These are not really separate plans, but all parts of an overall plan for information management. They are separated here to focus attention on specific elements.

The Long-Range Plan for Information Management. As was pointed out in Chapter 7, research indicates that organizations go through a six-stage process in developing an overall information management function (Nolan, 1979). The process starts with the first stage in which the computer is used for a specific low-level application, such as an accounting system, and ends at the sixth stage in which multiple applications are integrated into an information management environment. If Nolan's analysis is correct, information management in organizations, if allowed to mature, eventually leads to the sixth stage. Thus the long-range plan should outline how the organization will move from its present information management situation to the sixth stage. Although Nolan does not elaborate on the specifics of this sixth stage, other authors lead us to see it as encompassing the following:

1. Information viewed as a basic organizational resource.
2. Information recognized as a separate item in the organization's budget.
3. The assignment of the information management function to a high-level management-oriented person in the organization.
4. The establishment of a separate information service department.
5. The development of an integrated data base and a data base management system.
6. The development or purchase of a data dictionary system.
7. The gradual changing from systems that provide information for programmed decisions at the lower levels of the organization to systems that support programmed and nonprogrammed decisions at all levels of the organization.
8. A well-connected mix of centralized and decentralized processing systems.

The overall long-range information plan of the organization should contain timetables, estimated costs, technological requirements, milestones, go–no-go decision points, and measures of evaluation and success.

The Implementation Plan.   Although a broad-scope, long-range plan is necessary, a specific implementation plan is also crucial for any major applications such as installing an information system. Most planning mentioned in the literature is at this level. The implementation plan's purpose is to insure that the specific application meets the needs of the organization. Ein-Dor and Segev (1978c) see the implementation plan consisting of the following elements:

1. The development strategy.
2. The purpose of the system.
3. Priorities for choosing system functions.
4. System functions (applications).
5. Function goals.
6. Function requirements.
7. Documentation.

Ein-Dor and Segev (1978c) see these elements interacting in the following manner.

> The overall philosophy of development, or *development strategy*, sets the framework within which the process of MIS (Management Information System) strategic planning unfolds. Within this general concept, a unifying *purpose of the system* provides a sense of direction. This overall purpose plays a role in determining the *priority scheme for choosing between functions* which may potentially be included in the system. *Goals* are then established for each of the functions and, finally, these goals are operationalized as *requirements* or specifications. Each of these phases requires the creation of appropriate *documentation* both in order to direct the following stages of the process and for future reference. (p. 1633)

Paton and D'Huyvetter (1980) describe the implementation plan as a hierarchy of plans (see Fig. 10-1). Their description of the plans follows:

> 1. Project plan. The main plan is the project plan. It is usually based on a critical path schedule of task completion. It lists all major steps to be completed and all areas of responsibility for the people working on the project. All other plans are derived

Figure 10-1.   A Hierarchy of MIS Implementation Plans

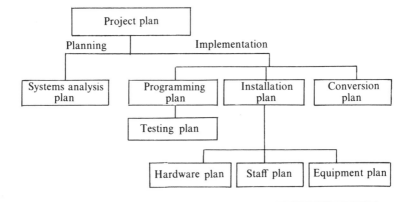

Note. From *Automated Management Information Systems for Mental Health Agencies: A Planning and Acquisition Guide* by J. Paton and P. D'huyvetter, U.S. Department of Health and Human Services, NIMH Mental Health Service System Reports (Series FN No 1), 1980, p. 63.

from the project plan. The project plan should be devised by the in-house MIS project team and the contractor if one is used. Once devised, it should be documented and submitted to the MIS advisory group for review and approval.

2. Systems analysis plan. This plan delineates every task to be completed as part of the systems analysis stage, defines milestones and completion dates, and indicates responsible personnel assigned to each task. Since the systems analysis stage is likely to be complex, this plan will actually be a compilation of numerous smaller plans corresponding to each functional subsystem.

3. Programming plan. This plan will be developed by the contractor or project team doing the software development and should be incorporated into the final contractual agreement between the agency and the contractor if outside services are to be used. It should be noted that while other tasks in the project plan may be pushed through with crash measures, this one can be achieved only by careful analysis and control. Programming takes time.

4. Testing plan. The testing plan must relate to the programming plan. For a system being developed from scratch, the amount of testing required and the costs of testing will likely be very high. The contractor or project team should be required to develop a plan indicating the segmentation of programming and testing and the corresponding time frames and costs.

5. Installation plan. The installation plan is actually a compilation of the hardware plan (hardware delivery and installation), the staff plan (hiring and training of operators and supervisors), and the equipment plan (ordering and receipt of office supplies and equipment necessary to support the MIS staff and the hardware). This plan should be approved by the administrator and the MIS advisory group as part of the final preparation.

6. Conversion plan. The developers should prepare a detailed plan for converting the old system to the newly developed one. The plan should provide for a period of parallel operation during which time the new system is observed in day-to-day operation. If there are numerous operational functions being mechanized, it is likely that individual modules will be converted rather than the entire system at one time. Whatever the case, conversion relies upon timely completion of the programming, testing, and installation plans. (p. 112)

The Organizational Adjustment Plan. Perhaps the most neglected planning is for the changes that must occur in the organization for it to accommodate an information management application. We have very little information on what organizational changes take place as a result of an information management application, especially for human service organizations. Besides the benchmarks listed in Figure 7-1, some of the organizational changes alluded to are as follows:

1. Power shifts to top management due to more accurate and timely information.
2. Power shifts to those who understand and use the information management system.
3. Power shifts to those in linkage and boundary-spanning roles during the implementation process.

4. Decisions becoming centralized higher in the organization as more accurate data is available to top decision makers and the decisions become complicated by more information.

5. Decision making becoming more structured and less flexible because increased information focuses, quantifies, and rationalizes decisions.

6. Sections of the organization becoming more dependent on each other due to the development, updating, and use of a common data base.

Although these changes may not occur in all cases, the organization must plan to accommodate some essential changes if the information management application is to be a success.

Besides the organizational adjustments that occur over the several years of information system development, operation, and improvement, specific organizational adjustment must be planned for the implementation of each specific application. Appleton (1979b) discusses the organizational structures and roles which should accompany an in-house information management effort. He recommends the organization develop two parallel structures under the chief executive: the steering committee and its subcommittees, and the information services executive. To insure checks-and-balances, the steering committee's role in relation to the information services executive is similar to that of the United States Congress to the President. Whatever the structure, the point is that the organizational changes necessary for the implementation of any information management application should be planned and roles and duties well specified.

Ein-Dor and Segev, in analyzing what organizational variables lead to successful implementation, have developed a series of propositions, some of which point to the organizational adjustments that will increase the likelihood of a successful implementation. Some of their most relevant propositions are summarized below (Ein-Dor and Segev, 1978b, pp. 1071-1074).

1. Management information system success and allocation of sufficient resources are mutually dependent.
2. Organizations whose systems are formalized, quantified, and that produce data appropriate to their decision and control processes have a greater likelihood of successfully implementing a management information system.
3. Organizations whose management information system responsibility is placed in a separate high-level department have a higher likelihood of a successful management information system.
4. The likelihood of management information system success is increased by the appointment of a high-level steering committee.

Although these organizational changes are discussed in more detail later, they are mentioned here to illustrate the types of organizational planning that should occur.

The People Adjustment Plan.   The necessity of preventing resistance and promoting use is well recognized, but not commonly planned for. The people adjustment plan includes ways to decrease resistance, structure incentives, integrate the information management function into organizational activities, and develop indices of acceptance and use. (For additional information in this area, see Guideline 3, involving the user, and Chap. 11, the discussion under resistance.)

Guideline 2

Top-level commitment and involvement are necessary.

Moving an organization from one that is unconscious of information management to one that considers information as a basic resource and information management as a core function requires substantial organizational changes that only top management can bring about. Information management is basic to the organization's goals, objectives, policies, procedures, and processes, and thus will eventually involve top-level policy decisions. Designers and lower-level personnel cannot make these important decisions for the organization. Nolan's stages of data processing illustrate that the information management function moves higher and higher in the organization as information management develops and matures. Rather than reacting to this movement, it is advisable that top management lead this movement. Top management should perform the following tasks if it is to lead as well as demonstrate commitment and involvement.

Learning about Information Management. To begin, managers need to be able to approach information management from what Ein-Dor and Segev (1978b, p. 1073) term realistic expectations. Top-level managers must not be dazzled by technology they do not understand. Vendors and systems designers oversell, and top-level decision makers must be able to cut through the promises and jargon to obtain a realistic picture of what they can expect. This basic knowledge is essential if top management is to control the information management efforts. If not controlled, designers and consultants will develop systems that meet their own needs rather than the needs of the organization. Rarely is the technician or designer able to learn and understand the organization as easily as top management can learn the basics of information management.

Management must also understand the total change process that the organization will take in its attempt to manage information and realize that this process takes from 1 to 3 years before the real benefits begin to be felt. Top managers who have unrealistic expectations, such as rapid improvements due to the purchase of an information system, can only become frustrated and spread their disenchantment to the rest of the organization.

Securing a Stable Funding Source. A major task of top management is to secure a stable source of funding that will allow the development effort to proceed at a steady pace. An information management application, such as an information system, that suffers from inadequate or erratic funding will quickly lose the momentum and the commitment of the organization.

Identifying the Organization's Information Needs. The task of identifying information needs, although extremely difficult in the human services, "probably accounts for the downfall of more design efforts than any other factor except managerial participation" (Ross, 1976, p. 26). The task involves operationalizing goals and objectives and determining the data and information required to move the organization toward goal achievement. If the organization fails to ensure that the information the organization collects is geared toward its goals and objectives, all information management efforts will result in inadequate systems being developed. Carter and Newman (1976), in their discussion of data systems for a mental health center, list several series of questions an organization should ask itself to help determine its data needs (see Fig. 10-2). Few human services organizations presently are able to answer the questions posed by Carter and Newman.

Assigning Quality Personnel to the Information Management Effort. The task of assigning personnel to the information management function may be difficult considering the constraints caused by the scarcity of qualified personnel and, in government, the requirement of operating with civil service employees. A small human service agency may want to consider using an outside consultant to interview candidates since information management personnel are so critical to the development effort. A large human service agency may consider developing a separate nonprofit corporation to by-pass restrictions on hiring, salaries, and so forth, and to give the information management function the flexibility it requires.

Ensuring Available Training.   Training for system users and the whole organization is so critical that the responsibility should be assigned to a high-level employee and training money should be designated in the organization's budget. Most organizations budget for hardware, software, and maintenance, but not for training personnel to accept and use the system once it is developed. The old adage "garbage in—garbage out" is applicable to any information management effort. Unless personnel know how to supply the correct information, the system is doomed to failure.

Integrating Information Management into the Policies, Procedures, and Practices of the Organization.   As long as information management is not considered a basic function and integrated into the organization policies, procedures, and practices, the use and acceptance of this system will be in jeopardy. For example, new employees should understand the role an information system plays in the organization and the security with which it must be operated.

Promoting Trust.   An information system accumulates large quantities of sensitive information that allows for evaluation and control—for example, the ability to compare employees' performance or track employees' time and effort. Information is power and can be used constructively or destructively by top management. In order for employees to collect powerful information correctly, they must trust that the information will be used for goal achievements rather than for increasing management's power, personal gain, or for the punishment of particular employees.

Establishing Incentives for Using Information and Any Other Required Changes.   A good analysis to undertake

Figure 10-2.   Questions an Agency Data System Should Address

Questions Related to Services

1. Does your agency have a way of identifying the target population?

2. Does your agency have a way of expressing the degree of client impairment in terms of general levels of disability or dysfunction?

3. Does your agency identify an array of services according to (a) the target population(s) served, and (b) levels of functioning?

4. Has your agency identified complementary services that could have an impact on the clients you are serving?

5. Has your agency analyzed the coordination of its array of services for each target population with complementary services offered elsewhere in your community?

Questions Related to the Management of Services

1. Can you substantiate a client's assignment to a level of functioning by some objective criteria?

2. Does your program have a systematic procedure for setting a timed sequence of intermediate objectives and long-term goals for each client and for relating these sequential objectives and goals to the client's level of functioning?

3. Does your agency have a systematic way to assign a planned sequence of services or therapeutic activities to accomplish intermediate objectives and long-term goals?

4. Does your agency maintain an updated record of service contacts that show: (a) client's level of functioning, (b) type of service rendered, (c) amount of service (time), and (d) who delivered the service?

5. Does your agency have a regular review process that could be used to ascertain (a) that services planned have been delivered, and (b) that client progress is occurring as expected?

Questions Related To Cost Accounting

1. Does your agency have some criteria by which to distinguish between direct service costs and indirect costs?

2. Do members of your agency regularly report their indirect service activities relating to each target population?

3. Does your agency summarize the amount of each type of direct and indirect service delivered by various categories of personnel?

4. Does your agency keep records of expenditures that permit you to estimate direct costs per hour of service delivered?

5. Does your agency have a method for allocating or prorating indirect service expenditures to each hour of direct service?

6. Does your agency have a procedure for calculating expenditures for each client served?

Questions Related to Program Evaluation

1. Does your agency have a policy for determining what information is appropriate for making decisions at various operational and administrative levels?

2. Does your agency use cost and outcome information to discover and solve problems in the service delivery system?

3. Does your agency regularly use procedures to test alternative solutions to service problems and to translate the results into program decisions?

4. Does your program assess the reliability and validity of the information used to manage and evaluate your program?

Note. From *A Client-Oriented System of Mental Health Service Delivery and Program Management: A Workbook and Guide* by D. E. Carter and F. L. Newman, U.S. Department of Health, Education, and Welfare, National Institute of Mental Health, Publication No. (ADM) 76-307, 1976.

occasionally is to examine whether the incentives in the organization are in line with the behaviors desired—in this case, the use of computerized information in decision making. For example, is it easier for employees not to use the information than to use it? Is use rewarded, that is, is use a part of the employee's performance appraisal? Are those who resist change given more attention and consideration than those who cooperate? Correcting the organization's incentive system can go a long way in helping the desired changes occur.

Demonstrating Involvement and Commitment. Modeling the behavior expected by others is extremely difficult. It requires leading rather than lagging behind, making timely decisions and being willing to handle quickly the conflicts that change inevitably generates. Attendance at key meetings may not be required for other than an obvious show of support.

The thread running throughout all these tasks is that top management must be able to commit itself and demonstrate that commitment by involvement. Involvement means hard work, and with information management the rewards are not immediate or as apparent as with other efforts. As organizations move from a single application to an information management environment, however, the tasks must be done, and success depends on top-level management becoming a willing leader rather than a reluctant follower.

Guideline 3

Involve the potential user in all phases of the process.

Involving the user is another guideline on which all agree. Not only does involving a potential user from the earliest effort provide a valuable educational experience, but it opens communication, reduces unrealistic system design, reduces fear and resistance, secures commitment, and helps insure future use. Users are seen as those who come into contact with the system by either supplying the information, operating the system, or using the results.

Involving the user is based on the common principle in human services of citizen participation. As with citizen participation, it is difficult and time consuming, but an essential process.

As was pointed out in Chap. 7, the involvement process varies by each stage of implementation. The potential user may be involved by a variety of steps. Some of these are as follows:

1. Orient the system to the user's needs—for example, the reduction of paperwork.
2. Expose staff to a positive similar experience as early in the process as possible; for example, visit successful systems or bring in speakers of different professions (social workers, psychologists, managers) from successful efforts to share their experiences.
3. Provide training for the potential users and new employees.
4. Make it easy, enjoyable, and nonthreatening for users to interact with the system and familiarize themselves with its capabilities—for example, encourage staff to play computer games such as "Doctor" and "Star Trek."
5. Make user involvement, acceptance, and use a criteria in personnel performance evaluations.
6. Periodically look at the rewards the implementation process has for involvement, acceptance, and use. Present policies and practices may punish rather than reward the users for their positive efforts.
7. Include the system and its use in the standard operating procedures of the agency.

8. Protect those who could be potentially harmed or lose status or power due to computerization—for example, prefer retraining and attrition to displacement or replacement.

9. Provide for early payoffs from the system; for example, a simple personal biorhythm chart was a psychological boost to one user because it was his first tangible evidence of the computer's capabilities after months of restructuring his records and inputting volumes of information into the system.

10. Make the system usable. The decision support system concept—that is, a system that is interactive, conversational, and tolerant of errors—is especially applicable for human service personnel who typically do not have information management or computer training in their background.

Guideline 4

Communicate frequently, through many channels, and in multiple formats.

During any implementation effort, information should be repeated often using multiple channels and formats. Some people read memos, others newsletters or bulletin boards, while others gain their information through formal or informal meetings. To be effective, communication must be tailored to the variety of receivers rather than requiring all receivers to respond to one form of communication.

Effective communication is essential if system designers and users are to understand each other's needs. Communication must be a continuous process as designers interpret what they think the users are saying into the requirements of the system and users react to the designers' developments. Free-flowing communication plays a self-correcting role crucial to a well-designed system.

One of the first steps that should be taken is to circulate a list of definitions of the jargon of all parties involved, since human service personnel, systems, and computer personnel speak mutually incomprehensible languages. Another way to open channels of communication between system designers and users is simply through physical proximity. If the system designers are given an office isolated from the rest of the organization, interactions will be difficult. A central location and encouragement by management through proper introductions and small parties at significant benchmarks in the development effort, for example, the computer installed and operating, will help make the organizational climate more conducive to open communication.

One of the most useful forms of communication is the forewarning of impending changes before the changes take place. Forewarning increases involvement, generates ideas, reduces resistance and dispels rumors. For example, the following should be presented and discussed with all involved.

1. It will take at least a year before the benefits of most applications become evident. Minor system efforts take approximately 1 year to implement and test out. Major efforts take 3 or more years.
2. The work load of everyone will probably increase during the implementation period.
3. It may be necessary to shift organization structure and strategy during the implementation period, because different strategies and approaches work best during each phase of the implementation process.
4. If a change does not work, it may be necessary to change back. This trial-and-error process may be frustrating, but it is necessary.
5. Extra training will be needed by all.

Communications should not be considered only an in-house function. Most human service agencies have boards, interested citizens, and clients who need to be informed. The local press can be used to communicate with the public and to give the agency some publicity for its efforts to improve services. This publicity can also help boost employee morale.

Guideline 5

Establish a high-level steering committee.

It is commonly acknowledged that a high-level steering committee increases the likelihood of success of a major application. A high-level committee should be composed of department leaders who can act as the go-between and communications conduit between the organization and the system designers. They should have high-level status and be able to handle the power that eventually gravitates to such a boundary-spanning role.

The top-level steering committee is a psychological symbol of top management's commitment to the implementation effort as well as a means to identify specific individuals within the organization who are entrusted with the responsibility for the application's success. Their function can include that of planning for and monitoring the information management application, approving work plans and system designs, and establishing information management policies and procedures. However, they should avoid unofficial conflict resolution and the temptation to solve some of the problems that are uncovered in the process of implementation. These conflicts and problems should be disassociated with the application if possible and handled through traditional organizational channels. In handling conflicts, the committee should deemphasize the individual and stress the overall guiding principles.

Guideline 6

Assign information management to a separate top-level
department.

Although the advisability of information management operating from a separate top-level department has been mentioned several times before, it deserves mention as a separate
guideline, for as Ein-Dor and Segev (1978b) point out,

> The likelihood of a successful MIS effort declines rapidly the
> lower the rank of the executive to whom the MIS chief reports,
> and is virtually negligible if the executive responsible is more
> than two levels below the chief executive of the particular
> organization which the MIS serves. (pp. 1073-1074)

Creating a separate top-level department is not what
usually occurs in most organizations. The tendency is to
locate the information management function in the department of first application, and create a separate high-level unit
only when the first application proves viable and other
applications are being added. This practice conceals a serious
trap as Gibson and Nolan (1974) point out,

> The department that controls the resource becomes strongly
> protective of it, often because a manager or a group within it
> wants to build up power and influence. When the time comes
> for computing to assume a broader role, real conflict arises—
> conflict that can be costly in terms of management turnover
> and in terms of lingering hostilities that inhibit the provision of
> computer services and applications across functional areas. (p.
> 80)

The top-level department helps the information services
executive cope with the power and controversy that accompany most data management applications and adds the
additional protection and insulation an information services
executive may require.

> The experience of many suggests that the MIS manager and senior management think in terms of a 3-year contract for the position, with explicit recognition that there will be organizational pressure to push out the MIS manager. (Gibson & Nolan, 1974, p. 87).

Guideline 7

Plan for modular design and gradual change.

As the discussion on the necessity of information management planning (Guideline 1) indicated, information management is a long-term effort. Because it is also a complex process, the changeover should be gradual and the design modular. A persistent warning is to avoid implementing the grand design.

Because information management in the human services is still in its infancy and few proven systems exist, gradual implementation makes sense. It avoids a large commitment, spreads out the cost and risk, is less chaotic, and, most important, it gives the organization the time needed for self-education and adjustment to any new system.

When developing a system from relatively independent modules, initial conceptual work on the total system should be completed in order to develop modules that will eventually tie together to form a network of modules or a total system. The most difficult conceptual work involved is defining systems, boundaries, and interfaces, and in viewing the system as an integral component of agency decision making. Too often this initial conceptual work is avoided and with unfortunate consequences. A module purchased or developed without this conceptual work may have to be changed substantially when another module is added.

In deciding which module of an information system to implement first, the agency has several alternatives. First, it can computerize its most pressing data need or those needs that are presently most difficult to handle by hand—for example, large volumes of client data. Second, it can choose to computerize data and information that address the most pressing agency decisions to be made, such as program evaluation. Finally, it can computerize data and information in one of the most stable systems in the agency and one in which the appropriate data are clearcut—the payroll. The basic considerations in these alternatives are how much experience the agency has with computers, how developed the present manual information system is, and how much risk the agency can afford to take. If the agency has experience with computers or access to computer expertise, and its data are presently conceptualized in a way that addresses basic agency goals, then the agency may be willing to computerize a module that affects major agency decisions or automate a major agency function. If these conditions do not exist, then computerizing one of the most stable agency subsystems is a safer way to begin. Once the initial application is completed, the agency will be better prepared for more difficult applications, such as areas where there is considerable conceptual disagreement and where the information can have a profound effect on agency decisions.

Guideline 8

Separate information management changes from other
organizational changes.

Too often, implementing an information management application is seen as a chance to accomplish some other long-overdue organizational change. The overdue change should be made first, and then an information management application developed to support the new structure (Lucas, 1978, p. 318). Lumping changes together results in generalizing the resistance associated with the other changes onto the information management application and possibly jeopardizing its implementation and use.

Guideline 9

Document what you do.

Documentation is one of the least desirable tasks and is easily overlooked, for there are few immediate payoffs. However, it is an essential task throughout all the stages of any information management effort. As Ein-Dor and Segev (1978a) point out,

> One of the most significant factors differentiating companies which are effective information system users from those which are not is the quality and content of their written plans. Thus despite its seeming technical appearance, this is an issue to which management is well advised to address itself. (p. 63)

Documentation helps tie the system modules together. It is the basis for evaluating and controlling the system effort as well as the building of additional applications on the existing system. It is also the key to continuity, especially when technology is rapidly changing and knowledgeable personnel change jobs frequently. Documentation is often neglected because its value is not immediately visible to managers and it is a boring task for system designers.

Concluding Remarks

The trend running throughout these guidelines is that the typical organization spends almost all its time on the technological aspects of an application while the areas that need the most attention are the overall planning of the system and the adjustment of the people and the organization to the change. These guidelines also indicate that information management is a complex process and still evolving. It is no easy task for an organization.

Chapter 11

LIMITATIONS AND PROBLEM AREAS

Introduction

This chapter discusses the limitations and problems associated with computer-based information management applications and their implementation. Although most of the research and experience have been with management information systems, the limitations and problem areas apply in some respects to any computer-based information management application.

Some overlapping information may exist between this chapter and the previous chapter on guidelines. It exists because the guidelines, if followed, are by definition intended to minimize the limitations and prevent the problems from occurring in the first place. However, an attempt has been made to prevent overlapping information unless the different focus of this chapter adds additional understanding to the information presented.

Limitations

Limitation 1

Good management is a prerequisite for information management.

Information management considers information a tool to be used in decision making. It is a very powerful tool, but one totally dependent on sound management practices before it can be used. As Ross (1976) points out,

> If good planning and control does not exist within the frame-work of a good organizational structure, no degree of sophistication with a computer is going to cure the basic ill. MIS (Management Information Systems) must be built on top of a management system that includes the organizational arrangements, the structure and procedures for adequate planning and control, the clear establishment of objectives, and all the other manifestations of good organization and management. (p. 23)

The organization must be ready to use any information management application. This readiness is psychological as well as structural. Wilson (1966) has pointed out the psychological readiness by indicating that successful and failing organizations are most likely to benefit from any computerization effort. Successful organizations can best withstand the changes associated with an information management effort, whereas failing organizations must change or risk termination.

Structural readiness has been called "organizational maturity" by Ein-Dor and Segev (1978b, pp. 1071-1072). They see a mature organization as one in which systems are formalized and quantified, data are available that are appropriate to the organization's decision and control processes, and the sociopolitical structure is rational and compatible with the information system development. Although good information management may enhance organizational maturity, it cannot change an organization that is not mature into one that is. What exists is a symbiotic relationship between sound management and information management. Sound management is dependent on information management and information management is dependent on sound management. This limitation is especially applicable for the human services in which goal specification, quantification of processes and outcomes, and clear specified control mechanisms are many times nonexistent. Human services are a mix of centralized and decentralized controls and payment to agencies is usually based on whether services are rendered, not on client movement toward some clearly defined commonly accepted goal. It is a system in which the consumers, due to the nature of their problem—for example, mental illness and mental retardation—have not demanded the necessary quantification and controls. Given the nature of the human services, the maturity Ein-Dor and Segev talk about is difficult to obtain.

Limitation 2

The inclusion and exclusion of data.

The data included in any information management application take on increased importance whereas data excluded from the system become irrelevant. When setting up an information management effort, the difference between a piece of data or information included and excluded may be minimal, and in some cases a completely arbitrary decision must be made. Once in the system, however, the data item takes on increased importance because it is used in multiple decision making throughout the organization. Data excluded cannot be used unless a separate data collection effort is mounted. In addition, once a piece of data is included in a system, it becomes extremely difficult to remove or change because of the reprogramming required and because of the destruction of trend data of which the data element is a part.

This limitation becomes especially important for data and information used in the control or monitoring function. For example, one piece of information on which vocational rehabilitation counselors have been monitored and evaluated was the number of clients who successfully completed the program. The result was that rehabilitation counselors increased their performance rating by a process known as "creaming," or choosing only the best candidates or those who could get through the program in a short period of time and with minimum expenditures. Clients with multiple problems and handicaps were not brought into the program because it was difficult to show success with such clients. Similarly, employment services that are evaluated on the number of job applicants who report for a job interview may make many referrals to show progress, even though they know the applicants have no chance of being hired. The end result is a dramatic rise in referrals which on paper looks like success but which may, in fact, anger potential employers and result in overall program failure. This limitation is accentuated in human services because our unit of service and our measure of client movement are extremely hard to quantify (see the discussion in Chap. 1 under Quantification of Services). The problem is that key activities are often left out of an information system simply because they are hard to quantify.

Defining what data to include and exclude from an information system becomes one of the crucial tasks an agency must undertake. Some authors suggest an agency start automating information that relates to the major agency decisions that must be made to achieve its goals. Others suggest automating based on the reports an agency must produce. Carter and Newman (1976) recommended an agency examine or be able to address certain key questions relating to services, management accounting, and evaluation (see Chap. 10, Fig. 10-2). Given the turbulent nature of human service agencies, all three approaches should be examined with the following considerations.

First, an agency need not do away with all paper files. If keeping a file by hand is easy and is causing no problems, then automating it may not be necessary unless the data are important in combination with other data elements. Certain data and files lend themselves to automation and others do not. Those that lend themselves to automation are those containing large volumes of data with the same format that are frequently searched, manipulated, or rearranged. Second, as mentioned above, data take on increasing importance simply by being in the system. Tenuous data may be viewed as ironclad facts by those mystified by computers or those working in agencies unfamiliar with the data's limitation, for example, planning bodies. Third, the easiest data to computerize may not be the most useful for decision making. The easiest data to computerize are internal routine data at the operational or middle-management level, whereas the most pressing data needs involve the client-worker interaction or those concerning the agency's environment. Finally, people tend to collect more information than they need. Although psychological studies point to the additional security the unused data give to decision makers, keeping unnecessary data is expensive and time consuming. With this point in mind a cost-benefit analysis should be conducted before automating all data whose use is not obvious.

Limitation 3

Developing a good information system will not insure its proper use.

In the final analysis, an agency information system is the user's system. They make or break any effort in information management by using the system or avoiding it. Use is also discussed in Chapter 10 and in this chapter under the problem area of resistance.

Although not using the information system can be a major problem, an equally severe problem is overreliance on the system. At this point in their development, agency information systems are able to capture only a portion of the information needed in agency decision making. Information systems tend to automate only that information which is easy to collect and computerize, regardless of whether the information is the most pertinent for decision making. Similarly, information systems up to this point have collected information on only the formal activities of an organization. The conceptual framework and research necessary to allow an information system to process meaningful information on the informal organization do not exist. As research from the Hawthorne studies of the late 1920s onward has pointed out, the information of the informal organization is equally important in decision making as the information of the formal organization (George, 1972). Finally, information systems have difficulty addressing the data connected with the external environment, one of the major determinants of agency decisions. Until information systems can begin to capture better information, especially from the informal organization and the organization's environment, the output will not have, and should not have, the impact that many designers and proponents have in mind. An information system does not replace the need to use other decision making aids, such as a political analysis of the situation or intuitive judgment.

Limitation 4

The inability to determine the cost benefit is problematic.

A severe limitation at this point in time is the inability to determine the costs and benefits associated with any information management application. One of the consequences of viewing information as a resource is the necessity to cost out information in the organization's budget and to weigh those costs against the likely benefits the organization will receive from the information in the future. In human services, as with many other organizations, this is an almost impossible task at present. We simply do not yet have the experience or tools. At this point, all we can say is that computer-based information management applications have been very costly in terms of money, frustration, time, and effort, but that they improve the quality and systematization of what is done to such an extent that organizations are continuing to use them more and more. Little evidence exists to show that information management applications reduce cost, personnel, or paperwork.

Cost-benefit analyses are extremely difficult to do. The problem in performing a cost-benefit analysis stems from the difficulty of placing a dollar figure on the obvious and hidden costs and benefits in general and of computerized information in particular. Figure 11-1 presents some of the obvious and hidden costs and benefits associated with information management. Not only is it impossible to cost out some of the obvious and hidden costs and benefits, but costs and benefits vary depending on the present level of computerization, the level of systemization that presently exists, the rate of implementation, the reliability demanded of the system, the mode of operation, the number of applications in the system, the sophistication of the system, and the security demanded.

It is important to recognize the problem of determining cost benefits, because too often computer-based information management applications are sold to agency managers by a vendor, and subsequently by the agency manager to the board and staff, as a labor, cost, or paperwork-saving device. The result is job insecurity by those who feel they could be replaced, high unrealistic expectations, and eventual frustration and resistance as the system faces its first cost overrun

Figure 11-1.   Costs and Benefits Associated with Information Systems

	Obvious	*Hidden*

Costs	Computer hardware
	Computer software
	May require new staff
	Supplies
	Space and storage
	  equipment
	Design of the system
	Programming of system
	Electricity
	System maintenance
		Disruption during
		  implementation
		Disruption due to system
		  failure
		Personnel training and
		  education
		Staff displacement
		Extra work to put in system
		Loss of work effort and
		  quality due to frustration
		  and change
		Time and effort needed to
		  overcome conflict and
		  resistance
		Running new and old
		  system simultaneously to
		  insure accuracy

Benefits	Increased accuracy of
	  routine tasks (payroll)
	May reduce future staff
	  needs
	Quick access to data
	  and information
	Improved decision making
	More accurate data and
	  information
	Greater control over
	  agency operations
	Better research and
	  evaluation capacity
	Performs manipulations of
	  data previously
	  impossible (simulations)
	Ease of answering special
	  data inquiries and reports
		Frees workers from more
		  routine tasks
		Improved quality of
		  services
		Possible revenue increase
		  from more accurate
		  billing system
		Improvement of image or
		  competitive position
		  (Title XX contracts)
		Documents many processes
		  and systems previously
		  undocumented
		Helps integrate agency
		  services
		Better communication and
		  relations with the
		  community due to more
		  current and accurate
		  information

or requires preparing paperwork for the old as well as the new system during the implementation phase. The selling point of an information system is that it will allow the agency to do a better and more accountable job and may hold down future costs. Some authors feel that it is not necessary in the human services to conduct a strict cost-benefit analysis. Herzlinger (1977) indicates,

> Since most nonprofit organizations seriously underfund their information system activities, it is unrealistic and unnecessary to justify installation of a new design on a cost-savings basis. Rather, they should be justified on benefit-cost reasoning—that is, that the benefits of the system will exceed its cost. And the design phase should include meritorious documentation of these costs. (p. 86)

The key point of Herzlinger is that it is misleading for an agency that is presently spending little or nothing on information management to look at the cost and benefits of a major application such as an agency information system. Also most information management applications do not result in immediate benefits as cost savings and staff reduction, but reasoning indicates they will eventually result in more productive services and future cost avoidance.

Problems

Resistance

One of the major problems in implementing an information management application is resistance. This resistance seems more ingrained in the human services than in other organizations. It seems imbedded in human services personnel from the top levels of HHS on down to the casework level.

Consider, for example, the following quotes:

> Another problem encountered by the administrators and systems designers engaged in the application of information systems technology to human services has been the unusually stiff opposition from professional social workers who feel that technology is "dehumanizing" by nature and therefore detrimental to their basic service objectives. (Bowers & Bowers, 1977, p. 2)
>
> Administration of mental health services have typically been grounded in intuitive, unsystematically derived decision making by individuals whose training has not acknowledged the importance of the administrative role. These decisions have been less a function of planned and objective data collection and more a function of the political and professional value system of the clinician-turned-administrator. (Davis & Allen, 1979, p. 225)
>
> Indeed, some managers of nonprofits view their lack of quantitative skills as a rather endearing imperfection—like having freckles. Many of these managers were initially professionals who carry with them the culture and attitudes of the professional, including strong resistance to quantitative measures of their organizations' activities. They argue, sometimes persuasively, that professional work is too complex and diffuse in its impact to be easily accounted for and that naive attempts to account for its outcome might undermine the credibility and integrity of the work itself. (Herzlinger, 1977, p. 84)

Resistance to computerized information management applications is usually seen as deeply rooted in the human service professional's nature or developed due to the threats to status, ego, autonomy and control, or job security. Although these may be factors, resistance may also stem from the lack of exposure to a well-functioning system. State and federal systems have been the primary exposure of most human service professionals to any information management effort. State systems, however, are extremely complex and difficult to implement and are usually not model systems. The local human service professional has often had no say in the design of these systems and, as a result, the systems are primarily designed around state and federal problems and decision making. Few state and federal systems provide useful information to the agency worker in a timely manner and in a format that allows it to be readily used. The only role of local human service professionals has been to take the extra time to fill out the additional paperwork needed for the system. Thus most state and federal systems are resented because they represent extra paperwork with very little benefit to human service workers. On the community level, exposure of human service personnel to successful information management efforts has been hampered due to the absence of a human service delivery system in which to locate any information management effort. Consequently, resistance to information management systems by human service personnel is often due to a total lack of exposure to how a well-functioning system can help workers improve the services they deliver.

There are numerous ways to overcome resistance: for example, to forewarn of impending changes, to maintain open channels of communication, to increase user involvement, to make the system more usable, to deemphasize individual changes and stress the overall guiding principle, and to retrain rather than replace workers. All these have been elaborated on in previous sections.

Resistance comes not only from inside an organization but also from the agency's environment. For example, a local agency may have the maturity to implement an in-house information system, but cannot put the system in its budget because the funding agency sees it as a wasteful, unnecessary expenditure; or, the funding source, such as a local United Way, may see information management as a function it can perform for all member agencies, and will not fund any systems in competition to its own, no matter what the potential cost-benefit ratio.

Personnel

One of the most frustrating problems in information management is the lack of qualified personnel. The qualifications needed are composed of several usually separate disciplines. A vendor or consultant or an in-house information services executive should understand information management, computer hardware, software and peripherals, human services, agency management, and how to work with people in implementing change. Rarely are these qualities found in one individual, and few programs exist to educate this type of professional.

The personnel an agency needs vary with the three modes of operating an information management effort. Figure 11-2 presents three modes of operating an information management effort and the advantages and disadvantages of each mode. In the first mode an agency contracts out its information management effort. It uses limited in-house effort and expertise. This is the typical situation of many human service organizations with one application, usually bookkeeping, which is contracted out to a management or accounting firm. The problem in this mode is that little in-house education occurs and the agency is always at the mercy of the firm to insure that the information provided is worth the cost paid and the most efficient and effective methods are being used. Agencies usually do not have the expertise to reassess periodically the quality of the services they are receiving.

Another alternative is the joining of several agencies into a cooperative agreement and the pooling of limited resources to establish a cooperative service bureau. The problem with this mode, besides the boundary and territorial issues, is that any decision takes a cooperative effort and the information management personnel can use this lack of unified control to expand the information management function beyond the desires of the organizations involved.

Figure 11-2. **Advantages and Disadvantages of Three Operational Modes**

	Advantages	*Disadvantages*
Remote processing or service bureau	Costs vary with volume No equipment, space, maintenance, supplies, or new staff costs No overload problems Little training or technical expertise needed No long-term binding contract or commitment Easy transfer to in-house operation	Inflexibility Possible communication problems Employee turnover or changes at bureau Lack of control Lack of privacy and security May postpone in-house development
Cooperative agreement	Pooling of limited resources Transferability of applications Fosters cooperation and communication	Reaching agreement is difficult Lack of privacy and security Threats of withdrawal Lack of control
In-house	Adds additional expertise Maximum control Low turn around time and immediate access More responsive and flexible Fewer privacy problems Can cause needed changes More opportunity for involvement	Fixed costs no matter what volume Cannot handle overloads Breakdown and back-up problems Creates the need for more staff and another department Demands much time and effort

The final mode is in-house, and can be a totally in-house development and operation or a vendor development leading to eventual in-house operation. In purchasing the system from a vendor, the most pressing problem, besides quality personnel, is the long-term reliance on one or a few key individuals. The same problem exists for in-house development, for well-trained personnel are in short supply. The in-house person who is trained by the organization may be quickly offered a job by another agency. Another problem with in-house development is the control given to the designer, especially if documentation is not required. Without adequate documentation, firing the system designer could jeopardize the total information management effort.

A problem running throughout all three modes is the obvious proinformation management and technology bias of experts. Because their future career advancement is dependent on the growth of computer-based information management, they cannot be objective. Ross (1976, p. 20) indicates that most companies are overcomputerized by 20% due to the strong marketing of vendors and the strong bias of consultants and information management personnel. Danziger (1977, p. 31) mentions the tendency of computer personnel to overcomputerize during the initial installation and later on to use this overcapacity in nonessential applications and special studies simply to justify their existence.

Compounding the bias problem is the fact that little information is available to the agency to help overcome this bias. The academic community, a usual source of publications, has been left out of much of the information management activity in the human services because it is typically slow, inflexible, and structured along traditional disciplinary lines. Consultants have little incentive to share their expertise, since this expertise may be the competitive edge in getting the next contract. Because government is the primary funding source of the human services, most information at present exists in government documents. Sadly, however, many useful government reports are in-house publications with limited circulation. Many are not available through such traditional government sources as the U.S. Government Printing Office and the National Technical Information Service (NTIS).

To handle the personnel problems mentioned above, several good suggestions have been made:

1. Visiting similar agency applications on an educational basis and contacting a national association or local university for their advice.
2. Requesting the consultant by name, if possible, rather than simply specifying the firm.
3. Insuring plans are made for the possibility of changing key personnel.
4. Not letting the consultant make major decisions without involving the agency.
5. Having several consulting groups compete with each other. The debate this competition engenders will be an excellent educational device.
6. Considering the use of outside experts in the interview process, especially when inexperienced agencies are hiring personnel to lead the information management effort.
7. When choosing in-house personnel to head the information management effort, using stability, or the likelihood that a person will continue with the organization, as one of the criteria.
8. Making sure consultants have access to top management.

Centralization versus Decentralization

One of the core issues of management, that of centralization versus decentralization, takes on new dimensions with information management. Figure 11-3 presents several ways to view the centralization versus decentralization issue. Centralization and decentralization occur on all the dimensions in Figure 11-3, and any combination of centralization–decentralization is possible. The major determining factor, however, is computer hardware.

Figure 11-3. Ways to View the Centralization Versus Decentralization Continuum of the Information Management Function

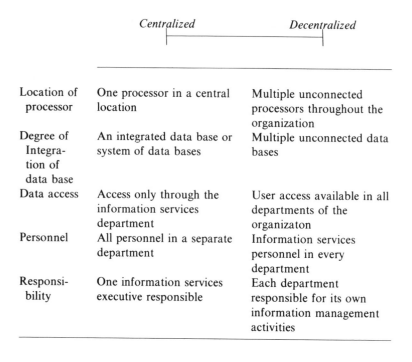

	Centralized	Decentralized
Location of processor	One processor in a central location	Multiple unconnected processors throughout the organization
Degree of Integration of data base	An integrated data base or system of data bases	Multiple unconnected data bases
Data access	Access only through the information services department	User access available in all departments of the organizaton
Personnel	All personnel in a separate department	Information services personnel in every department
Responsibility	One information services executive responsible	Each department responsible for its own information management activities

The issue of centralization versus decentralization is appropriate today more than ever because of the introduction of low-cost small microcomputers with substantial information-processing capacity. These small systems can be purchased by an individual or department and used as the basis of individual or departmental information systems, thus decentralizing the information management effort. The major advantages of a decentralized system is that it puts information management in the hands of those who use the system and increases use, training, and motivation. The major advantage of centralization is the ability to control or insure that the whole system functions in concerted suboptimization as discussed in Chap. 3.

The concept of distributed processing or the tying together of decentralized processing throughout the organization helps solve the centralization versus decentralization issue. If the total information management effort is tied together, the physical locations of the processing hardware, software, and the data base are meaningless from the user's perspective. That is, if users can access needed data conveniently no matter what their location, then it is inconsequential where the hardware resides, where the processing occurs, or where the data physically reside in this system. The key to distributed processing, then, is in developing a sophisticated data base management system that allows distributed data bases to be accessed as one integrated data base. The problem becomes one of combining, managing, and controlling all organizational data bases that are generated throughout a decentralized system. As was mentioned earlier, the integration and management of the individual or departmental data bases are major functions of the information services department. The key design question becomes how to reduce redundancy of data collection and storage yet increase access to all the data the organization has to offer. A data dictionary is one tool in this effort.

Although the issue of centralization versus decentralization is complex, the general advice is to centralize or decentralize based on the centralization or decentralization that exists in the organization's philosophy and structure. The goal is to match information management to the organization. As Nolan (1979, p. 120) points out in what he terms "data processing maturity," the structure of all information management applications should mirror the organization and its information flow.

Reliability

Although not listed as a major problem, reliability of the system is an important factor. If information management becomes a core organizational function, then a system break-down can cause major problems for the organization. The major question becomes how quickly and easily the system can be repaired and what to do in the meantime. Backup procedures and systems, and the periodic testing of these procedures and systems, should be a part of overall system design.

Technology Transfer

The area of technology transfer is important since human service organizations are latecomers to the use of informa-tion management technology, and the concept of transferring a system already developed seems a simple cost-reducing move. The analysis of technology transfer in government by Kraemer (1977) in Chapter 8 is particularly relevant for human service organizations; for as Bowers and Bowers (1977) concluded from their search of human service appli-cations, "virtually no record of successful transfers methods and procedures can be found" (p. 53). The conclusion must be that transferring computer systems developed in other settings is risky. Some warnings follow:

1. An organization should not try to customize or refine packaged software.
2. The best organization to accept outside computer systems is one that has already developed sufficient in-house expertise to evaluate and implement the outside system.
3. Technology transfer is an abrupt change that can increase resistance and prevent the gradual in-house learning and acceptance vital in assuring that the system will be used.
4. Cost savings are associated with technology trans-fers only when they (a) concern routine tasks; (b) are well documented; (c) are designed for transfer;

(d) are designed with cost savings in mind, rather than to advance the state of the art; (e) fit the agency's current computing capacity; (f) are self-contained; and (g) do not require frequent changes to update the system.

Upward Compatibility

In business each organization is seen as a separate competing entity. In human services each organization is seen as part of a total human service delivery system. Viewing the agency as a subsystem of a community human service delivery system raises the issue of upward compatibility of any system an agency develops. The question is whether the agency system will enhance or detract from the overall information management effort of the community service delivery system. The transfer of information outside the agency's boundaries thus becomes a concern in overall systems design. Upward compatibility can occur in terms of hardware, such as similar computers; software, such as similar languages; and similar data formats. The advantages of compatible systems include the ease of upward reporting, the establishment of community data bases for planning improved service delivery, and the ability to use other applications such as existing geocoding programs to change client addresses into census track or other geographic areas (Kluess & Moyer, 1978). The disadvantages of upward compatibility are that a system may become less responsive to internal needs as it adapts to the needs of a larger system. In addition, as Fried (1977, p. 30) and Boyd and Silver (Note 2, p. 31) point out, crossing internal and external agency boundaries multiplies problems and increases the chance of system failure.

Security and Privacy

Security and privacy are major concerns for human service organizations; for confidential client information that is not protected can result in injury to the client as well as loss of credibility by the agency. Security refers to the physical protection of hardware, software, file tapes, and so on. Privacy refers to the protection of information in the system. Typical security violations are intentional or unintentional modification or destruction of files, theft, fraud, sabotage, and private use of computer time. Privacy violations concern the improper access to and use of confidential information. The issue of privacy is intensified in a computerized system because of the computer's potential for quickly searching, organizing, and accessing large quantities of information.

Security and privacy problems result primarily if they are not part of the initial design and are only considered in reacting to a specific violation. The problem is exacerbated by the fact that human service personnel are unfamiliar with computer technology, and thus with the security and privacy issues and procedures associated wth computerized information. Small agencies are especially vulnerable, because their casual manner of operation may carry over into the security and privacy of computerized data. An additional problem is that laws have not kept up with technological developments and prosecution of violators is extremely difficult. Security and privacy concerns must be built into the system from the beginning and appropriate policies and procedures established and followed. For example, see the American Medical Association guidelines on confidentiality of computerized patient information (AMA, 1979). Technology is available as Roland (1979) illustrates, primarily because businesses, such as banks, have tremendous security and privacy problems and millions of dollars are at stake.

Access codes are the most frequent privacy protection. Access can be limited with codes that allow the user to either view, input, or change different subsets of information based on the user's level of authorization into the data base. Lower-level personnel may be limited to inputting new information only, and caseworkers may be authorized to view only their cases. Security is a matter of adequate locks, restricted physical access, duplicate storage, adequate procedures, fire protection, and so on. If services are contracted out, security and privacy must be discussed and assured by the vendor.

If proper designs are constructed and procedures established and followed, a computerized system can be as private and secure as any paper and pencil system. In fact, the concern over security and privacy has made many in-house systems a vast improvement over the previous security and privacy of the agency.

Evaluation

A problem area for the human services is that it is hard to evaluate the success of any information management application. As we have discussed earlier in this chapter, the traditional cost-benefit analysis is not very applicable to information management in the human services. A related problem is when to conduct a major evaluation, since the implementation of any information management application is an evolutionary process that may take several years. If the system is modular, an evaluation could be conducted after each major module is in place.

Ein-Dor and Segev's review of the literature (1978b, p. 1065) suggests the following criteria can be used in an evaluation as a measure of success: profitability, application to major problems of the organization, improvement of the quality of decisions made, improvement in performance, user satisfaction, and widespread use. They see use as the prime criteria and recommend a weighted average of all the criteria as a total evaluation measure. As can easily be seen, these measures are more appropriate for private profit-making organizations than human service organizations. Many, such as improved performance, are extremely hard to measure in the human services.

One simple way to evaluate is by examining whether the application went according to the expectations and purposes set out in the implementation plan. This is obviously an evaluation of the plan as well as the application and thus the evaluation mechanism becomes one way of perfecting the long-range plan and of controlling the total development effort.

Keen and Morton (1978, Ch. 8) suggest eight methods of evaluating a decision support system. These methods are briefly summarized below.

Decision Output.   The decision output method examines whether the system resulted in better decisions. The concept is laudable, but it is extremely difficult to separate out the effect of the information management application from the effect of the other changes that usually accompany the application, for example, the quantification of agency functions.

Changes in Decision Making.   The changes in decision-making method examines changes in how decisions are made regardless of the output. The rationale is that a better decision-making process means better decisions.

Improvement in the Decision Maker.   Improving the decision-maker method examines the changes that occur in the decision maker's attitudes toward and understanding of the decision process and its context due to an information management application. Measures in this area are virtually nonexistent.

Procedural Changes.   The procedural changes method focuses on the saving of resources as people, machines, paper, procedures, and routines. For example, an information system may result in the freeing of clerical time for other operations. These procedural changes are important because they relate to future cost avoidance. They say nothing, however, about improved agency performance.

Cost Benefit.   The cost-benefit method has been discussed previously.

Quality of the System.   The quality of the system method evaluates the system in terms of its accessibility, response time, reliability, data quality, documentation, and so on. It is a common method of evaluating a data management effort.

User Satisfaction.   The user satisfaction method assesses the user's feelings on the quality and success of the system.

Anecdotal Evidence.   The anecdotal evidence method consists of collecting insights, examples of success, testimonials, fortuitous events, and so on. This method is usually combined with hard data to round out the picture and to give a personal feel to successes and failures.

No matter which method is chosen, the important point is to view evaluation as the critical element of the overall plan. In addition, evaluation is not something done after the fact but something that must be included from the beginning of the information management effort if successful indices, such as use of the system, are to be collected from day one, or if pre- and postmeasures are used.

Unintended Effects

Any time a change is made to improve a system, that change itself generates new problems. Although computerized information systems are a tool that will help solve many of the information problems facing an agency, they generate their own set of problems. Solutions to these problems will undoubtedly generate a new set of problems, ad infinitum. As John Gall (1975) has pointed out, systems must be approached cautiously for they are deceptive and addictive. Gall states,

> Systems are seductive. They promise to do a hard job faster, better, and more easily than you do it by yourself. But if you

> set up a system, you are likely to find your time and effort now being consumed in the care and feeding of the system itself. New problems are created by its very presence. Once set up, it won't go away, it grows and encroaches. (p. 100)

What an information management application does is shift the problem area. The assumption is that this shift is toward less severe problems and in the best interest of the client.

A Rapidly Changing Market

Since change in the hardware and software market will continue the present rapid advancement for at least another 10 years, the tendency is always to wait until the next development hits the market before purchasing a system. Compounding the problem is the limited standardization that exists across manufacturers of computer systems, thus requiring vendors every 2 to 5 years to adapt their software to the cheaper computers to stay competitive. Given this state of flux, choosing a system can be compared to buying a car. It may be wise to buy a standard proven model from a reputable dealer rather than a high-performance system that may turn out to be one of a kind. Similarly, the agency may consider trading in computer hardware for a newer model while the old hardware still has considerable worth in the used computer market. The biggest risk is purchasing from a company that is being driven out of business by fierce competition. A reputable dealer is the best bet against this occurrence, unless an agency has the time and expertise to examine a computer manufacturer's stability.

Concluding Remarks

This chapter is by definition discouraging to anyone considering an information management application, for it focuses on the negatives. It can be considered similar to a news broadcast that is typically dominated by reports of problems and tragic events. A news program rarely puts all the negative information into the broader context. That is left to the viewer or listener. The same applies to this chapter. The reader must put the problems and limitations in their proper context.

The context in which this chapter must be read is that multiple problems and limitations exist in any organizational change; for example, program planning and budgeting systems (PPBS), or management by objectives (MBO). These problems and limitations, however, can be minimized if they are foreseen and precautionary steps taken. The problems and limitations associated with change do not negate the necessity of change, because not changing may have worse repercussions. What we should strive to do is to achieve well-planned and managed change, which in the long run improves the functioning of the system as a whole.

Part V

RECOMMENDATIONS FOR THE FUTURE AND A CAUTIONARY VIEWPOINT

Chapter 12 proceeds from the practical advice on information management given in Part IV to an examination of the future and a prescriptive set of recommendations on how human service professionals can prepare themselves for this future. Chapter 12 echoes the protechnology and optimism that is the overall tone of this book.

Chapter 13 takes a negative view of information management. It is a view not commonly found in information management literature. As with many high-specialty areas, most professionals who understand the technology well enough to take a critical look at its social impact are too wrapped up in it to stand back and take this cautionary view. Their careers are also invested in its continuation. It is with this cautionary view that the book is ended, for we must begin to analyze where our technologies are leading us, since once a direction is set, it is extremely difficult to change.

Chapter 12

THE FUTURE AND HOW TO PREPARE
FOR IT

The Future

As Chapter 1 pointed out, we are in the midst of an information revolution which involves the tying together of the computer and other information technologies. Predictions of the future of information technology and its use in organizations are extremely risky, for the market is volatile, as Amdahl (1978) indicates,

> For years we have been talking about the maturing computer industry. This would seem to imply an orderly, predictable environment wherein evolution has largely displaced revolution. Could anything be further from the truth? Despite the fact that computers have established a permanent niche, the basic product and range of applications are in turmoil. Computer manufacturers, large and small, continue to have at least the same level of concern that they have had in years past for the effectiveness and life of their products. (p. 18)

Nonetheless, there are certain directions that seem inevitable. Based on past and present trends, hardware is leading to the development of very large and very small systems that are powerful and usable. Information management in organizations appears destined to move towards maturity, that is, information management will be located in its separate top-level department and will be considered the core function of an organization. The information services department will provide the information needs of the whole organization by a highly integrated mix of centralized and decentralized data bases. The function of the information services department will be to capture the data the organization generates in its normal functioning and to develop the data into a flexible data base which will be the basis of all organizational decision making. Martino (1979) points to other applications that may become part of the information services department. They are summarized below.

1. Word processing, as discussed in Chapter 2.
2. Telecommuting, or the interaction with the work place by communications rather than in person.
3. Electronic libraries and reference searches. As more and more information becomes automated, it becomes possible to tap into the data bases of large libraries and browse or obtain local printed copies of needed materials.
4. Electronic mail, or the substitution of electronic media for the postal service.
5. Office calendars. If employee calendars are automated, the computer could schedule meetings by searching each participant's calendar for an appropriate time.
6. Electronic newspaper. The electronic newspaper could bring to the organization the latest offerings in news, weather, sports, and so on. Users, connected to the news media by a keyboard and video display, could program the computer to select only the information they need to stay up to date in their field.

7. Computer conferencing, or using the computer to structure, store, and process written communication among a group of people. Participants in a computer conference could type their message to conference members on computer terminals linked together by telephone. Members who are using their terminals at the same time could send messages directly. Members could leave the conference at any time without missing anything, however, since their messages would be stored with privacy codes and authorization levels. Resource banks, computer modeling, job banks, and other information can be a part of the conference program.

8. Networking, or the transmission of users' voice, video, or data by cable, optical fibers, or satellites. Video networks have been common on national news programs for years and are beginning to be cost-effective in the office setting.

As the applications above indicate, we will continue to move toward the automated office in which physical proximity is replaced by communications networks. As we continue to connect and merge information technologies with the computer and move from a paper medium to an electronic medium of communications, there will be less need for people in an organization to congregate in one central location (Vail, 1978). This move will become increasingly necessary as our present transportation system begins to collapse due to energy shortages and the demands for clean air.

Other more long-range changes are purely speculative and heavily dependent on technological inventions and innovations. Miniaturization has apparently not reached its limits. A 1978 *Time* article ("The Computer Society") points out that even the amoeba is a far smaller and far more powerful information processor than today's best chips and "if nature can do it, scientists feel challenged to try it, too" (p. 58).

There is considerable speculation on just how sophisticated machines can become. The debate on artificial intelligence—that is, can a machine ever possess intelligence or consciousness—requires that we take a hard look at what we define as intelligence and consciousness. Just as modern medical technology has destroyed the traditional boundary between life and death, so information processing via computers is blurring the concept of intelligence versus nonintelligence or consciousness versus nonconsciousness; for, is it intelligence if a machine with a human-developed data base can outperform man at work, such as diagnosing a patient, and at play, such as playing chess? Perhaps we need to accept computer-assisted intelligence as another form of intelligence that is useful in its own right. It seems that man's encounter with a new form of intelligence will not occur in outer space, as traditionally anticipated, but is presently occurring here on earth.

Some authors visualize computer-assisted intelligence more literally than figuratively. For example, Roland (1979) states,

> If a picoprocessor could be combined with memory of comparable speed and compactness, and the resulting picocomputer implanted in a person's skull and interfaced with the brain, that person could have more computer power than exists in the world today and all the stored knowledge of humanity as accessible as any brain cell. Such a thing could fundamentally change human nature, and is closer to realization than bionic limbs, organs, or senses. (p. 83)

Although Roland's computerized human may seem farfetched, what seems to be occurring is a merging of man and machine to perform tasks and to explore futures that man is totally incapable of alone. Just as industrialization saw machines performing many tasks and processes that man physically was not capable of performing, the information revolution will allow many mental tasks and processes that man is incapable of performing alone.

It is in this support relationship that computerized information management holds the most immediate promise for the human services. For example, with computerized data bases and other techniques, such as computer modeling, we may be able to improve the present primitive attempts to quantify the output of human services. We may also see the development of information systems that begin to support the most difficult decisions human service professionals face.

A fascinating step in this direction is catastrophe theory, which postulates that discontinuous events, such as prison riots and bridge collapses, can be predicted using computer-generated models. Thus the theory suggests that many seemingly discontinuous and random phenomena will follow the pattern of one of the seven 3-dimensional computer-generated surfaces (*Catastrophe*, 1976). Although catastrophe theory has not lived up to its proponents' predictions, it represents an attempt to combine computerized information management and mathematical modeling techniques to improve decision making in large unstructured situations.

Recommendations for Human Service Professionals

It is not a question any more of whether or not an agency should move toward computerized information management, but simply a question of when is the optimum time, what application to consider first, and how to proceed. This does not seem to be a pro-information management stance, just a statement of fact. Within the next 5 to 15 years, most human service agencies will develop one or more computerized information management applications. Human service personnel cannot afford to be outsiders or bystanders to these efforts, but must be active in developing and applying them.

The basic recommendations which follow involve ways for human service personnel to make up their lack of experience, knowledge, and research and become more in-

formed, objective, and realistic about the potential of information management in the human services. There are three
reasons why this is necessary. First, if human service personnel do not educate themselves on computer application, their
reaction will continue to be negative. This negative attitude
stems from the human service professionals' negative experience with large and bulky state systems and with their lack
of experience with smaller, more usable community or
agency efforts. This negative attitude puts the human service
professional in the position of resisting, avoiding, and oppos-
ing technological changes and preventing the use of information management applications to improve service delivery.

Second, if human service personnel do not become more
knowledgeable and experienced, the development and control of the agency's information management effort will be
left to other professions with less understanding of human
service agencies and of human services in general. As we
have seen, computerized information brings power to those
who know how to use it. If human service personnel lose the
power and control of the agency's information management
efforts, then the applications developed will not meet their
needs, and thus will not be sufficiently used and will not
result in improved decision making and improved services.

Third, planning is necessary if an agency is to move
from its first computerized information management application into a mature information management environment.
Only if human service professionals become knowledgeable
about information management can this planning occur. If
the planning does not occur, the agency will be forced by
events to move in the direction of information management
and will encounter the numerous problems that occur when
an organization moves in an unplanned direction it knows
little about.

Agency Personnel

Managers and direct practitioners must begin an education
process for themselves. This education process is a simple,

yet subtle and difficult process. What is needed is an awareness and a knowledge base so the agency can begin moving in the direction of considering information a basic manageable resource and plan for its development. If agency personnel are to be the primary users of information, they must determine what data and information need to be collected and how they are to be manipulated and presented. It is all agency personnel's responsibility to insure that agency information management efforts will contain the data and information that will lead to improved decision making. The manager's focus is usually on efficiency and accountability, the direct practitioner's focus is on effectiveness or improved services to clients.

The following steps, adapted from Schoech and Arangio (1979, p. 100), are recommended to achieve this neccessary knowledge base.

1. Begin to collect resources on the areas of information management, management information systems, systems, computers, quantification of services, change management, and so on. Maintain a file of terms, articles, knowledgeable people, organizations, and successful efforts.

2. Structure educational experiences such as conferences, continuing education courses, and lectures to local professional groups on subjects related to information management.

3. Occasionally visit a local computer or microcomputer shop and browse.

4. Use familiarity with information management and the specialized fields it encompasses as one criteria in hiring new staff.

5. Select one of the agency's next board or advisory committee members because of his or her expertise in information management.

The goal is not to develop human service personnel into computer programmers, systems designers, and so on, but

rather to develop human service professionals who can
understand the field of computerized information management well enough to plan for its application, and to retain the
necessary control over any application the agency imple-
ments. As Worthley (1978) points out,

> A manager's need for familiarity with the physical nature of the
> technology and its operations is minimal—enough so that he or
> she can cut through the jargon and mystique of the technician.
> Yet this minimal technical knowledge may be so critical
> that . . . "managers who fail to inform themselves . . . do so at
> their peril." (p. 291)

These are very difficult recommendations, for they require sacrificing valuable time and energy to begin a self-
education process that seems to satisfy little immediate need.
Professionalism, however, demands that agency personnel
become knowledgeable so they can use present concepts and
technologies to lead the agency into an information management environment.

Educators

The core responsibility of training human service professionals falls to our universities. It is in the bachelor's, master's
and doctorate degree programs that human service professionals must be exposed to information management and
their role in it. This is especially true for those who are
training to enter large human service agencies in which they
will eventually end up in middle- or upper-level management
positions. As Patti (1977) found in a survey of 90 managers
who were representative of several administrative levels in
public, quasi-public, and voluntary agencies,

> Survey findings indicate that competencies in the area of
> management information systems and program evaluation are
> essential, primarily because of the increasing importance that is
> being attached to accountability in social welfare agencies. (p.
> 10)

In checking with several master's degree-level schools of social work, one of the primary educators of human service personnel in the United States, it was found that courses concerning the use of computers, in other than a research setting, are rare and reach a very small percentage of those who graduate from these programs. These results are supported by an unpublished 1978 survey of schools of social work conducted by Dr. Gunther Geiss, Adelphi University School of Social Work, New York.

The gap between what education concepts and skills are needed and what is being offered in educational institutions is apparently one of the causes of the resistance and the refusal of human service personnel to accept the role of computerized information management in service delivery. Figure 12-1 presents the basic subject areas and activities to which all human service students should be exposed. It also lists advanced areas and activities for those students anticipating employment in a managerial-level position. Although human service educators should seek ways to develop more realistic and objective attitudes in their students, they must also decide to what extent they should educate those who will be in the forefront of the information management efforts that will occur in the future.

To aid educators in their efforts, we need research. The following are several examples of areas needing research.

1. What is the present attitude of human service personnel toward the use of computers in the human services? Can previous findings of "stiff opposition" be substantiated? If so, why do these attitudes exist and what are some of the ways to change them?

2. Are present conceptualizations of the human service delivery system adequate for applying and utilizing information management concepts? What do agencies need to do in order to develop a properly

Figure 12-1. Course Content to Acquaint Human Service Students with the Basic Knowledge, Skills, and Attitudes of Information Management.

I. Course Goal: To expose students to the terminology, concepts, and practices of information management

II. Basic Content Areas
   a. Viewing the agency as a system. Defining its subsystems and the community system of which the agency is a subsystem. Examining the goals, boundaries, environment, and interfaces throughout the system.
   b. Methods and techniques for the quantification and standardization of data and information associated with human service processes, practices, and outcomes.
   c. The decision-making process and ways to improve it.
   d. An overview of information management, its technological and organizational context, and its basic concepts, problems, and issues.
   e. Guidelines for a successful information management application.

III. Basic Course Activities
   a. Develop a glossary of relevant terms from the fields of systems, computer science, operations research, and human services.
   b. Visit a successful computer-based human service information management application.
   c. Hands-on interaction with a computer, for example, play computer games.
   d. Visit a microcomputer shop.
   e. Talk with computer hardware, software, or information system vendors or consultants.

IV. Advanced Content Areas (for those who will be human service managers)
   a. Managing organizational change.
   b. A discussion of data base designs, data dictionary systems, data base management systems, information systems, decision support systems and word processing systems.
   c. The consultation process and working with consultants.
   d. Flowcharting and team management and scheduling techniques, such as conflict management techniques and Gantt charts.
   e. Security, privacy, legal, and legislative constraints.

V. Activities for an Advanced Course
   a. Visit a business or government "mature" information management application.
   b. Develop quantification schemes for agency data in preparation for a computer-based information management application.
   c. Detail one or more of the following steps necessary to make major improvements in the information management of a real or hypothesized organization.
      1. The organization's preparedness to change and the feasibility of the application.
      2. Existing and future data needs and data flows.
      3. Alternate designs to improve present information management and the cost benefit of each design.
      4. The planning which must accompany the effort.
      5. The specifications of the chosen system.
      6. Security and privacy techniques and guidelines.
      7. The implementation and evaluation schedules and techniques.
      8. The organizational changes which must accompany the effort.

functioning and accountable delivery system? What data and information should they collect, how should it be organized, what monitoring and control mechanisms are needed, what agreements are necessary with other agencies, and with funding sources?

3. What professions should educate specialists in human service information management? What are the immediate and long-term effects of placing management and computer professionals in controlling positions in human service agencies? Do value and power conflicts usually occur, and are those conflicts a healthy or a destructive influence, for example, do services improve or suffer as a result?

4. What are the effects of different computerized information management applications on the human service delivery system? If an agency decides to implement a computerized application, before and after measures could do much to document the impact on the agency.

Universities are the logical places for this research to occur. Many students must complete a research project to graduate. Research related to computerized information management has fallen behind developments in computer technology and shows no sign of catching up. Without research, the present trial and error method will continue with a minimum of learning from our mistakes.

The area of research is especially complex. The field of information management is changing at such a rapid pace that today's research and theories may not apply to tomorrow's computers and their applications. Another difficulty is that an information management application is seldom complete. Applications are usually a continuous process, constantly changing, growing, and evolving. No two applications seem to follow the same pattern, since an almost infinite number of combinations of hardware, software, and application situations exist. Lawler (1977) describes an experimental approach, called "adaptive research," which is well suited for this type of research. Lawler states,

> A strong case can be made for the vital importance of assessing the relative effectiveness of different management practices and organization designs by studying what happens when they are introduced into organizations . . . . Adaptive research requires a comprehensive set of standardized measures, a number of sites so that meaningful comparisons can be made, a long time period, a third party, and careful assessment of the nature of the change. Research that meets these requirements . . . takes a large investment of time and effort, but this investment seems small in comparison to the importance of the questions which can be addressed. (p. 584)

Another example of a viable research approach is illustrated by Ein-Dor and Segev (1978b, pp. 1064-1077) who have taken the organizational context variable in Mason and Mittroff's definition of an information system and researched the literature to see under what organizational context an information system results in success. They break organizational context down into uncontrollable variables, such as size and structure; partially controllable variables, such as resources and psychological climate; and controllable variables, such as rank and location of the responsible executive. They then develop propositions that postulate when the interaction of these variables leads to successful implementation. This same process could be used for the other Mason and Mittroff variables, such as problems addressed and mode of presentation. The ultimate goal is to develop the interaction not only within the categories of the variables, but between each of the variables.

In summary, the response needed by educators is threefold:

1. Exposure of human service personnel to basic concepts and their application.
2. Conceptual development of human services as an accountable and productive system and the role of data and information in this system.
3. Research on the effects of using computerized information management systems in social service delivery and on the effects of different disciplines in controlling the computerization effort.

Others

Many tasks need to be completed that are beyond the capacity of individuals and agencies. These tasks fall under the responsibility of such human service personnel as regional, state and national planners, evaluators, funding sources, policy makers, and professional and client associations. They are necessary for the orderly and systematic use of computerized information management applications in the human services. Some of these tasks are discussed below.

Uniformity and Standardization. Uniformity in human service agency system development must be encouraged to prevent further entrenchment in the fragmented system that already exists. If standardization does not exist, each agency will computerize a different system with different definitions and different meanings for service units. The requirements of a decentralized community human service delivery system are similar to those Spangle (1978) indicated were required for a distributed information system.

1. A unified language.
2. Standardized procedures.
3. Correlation of the contents and structure of the distributed data base.
4. Operation of a common message delivery network (p. 17).

Developments in each of these areas are needed; for example, a state of the art study of human service definitions, boundaries, and interfaces would be extremely valuable. An international perspective would help prevent future definitional problems. As we have seen in our discussion of service integration, the coordination of human service data bases will be one of the most difficult tasks facing human service decision makers in the community in the years to come.

Research. It is necessary that research be conducted or sponsored. Experimental efforts should always be accompanied by pre- and postmeasures to determine the effect on the agency—for example, power redistribution, organization structural changes, cost savings, and service improvements. Here relatively simple and inexpensive studies could begin to fill a real research void.

Guidelines need to be developed on cost-benefit formulas or matrices for any information management application. These guidelines could be a valuable aid in separating out the obvious and hidden costs occurring in different types of effort and then pulling the information together to obtain some form of overall cost-benefit estimate.

Privacy guidelines and criteria are needed. Small agencies are particularly vulnerable and do not have experience or expertise in this area.

Guidelines are needed on how to choose and use a system designer, whether it be a vendor, a consultant, a university, or an in-house operation.

Techniques and methods are needed to allow an agency to evaluate its information management application, and evaluation must become an acceptable item in the budget request for information management funds.

Applications that lend themselves to nationwide development and standardization need to be developed. For example, a medication management information system would be a valuable clinical aid that could be developed and updated nationally and distributed to local agencies. Automated databanks on treatment literature and research abstracts could also be a standardized application. The list of similar needs is long and their use throughout the United States should gradually escalate as agencies begin to buy their own computers.

Involvement of the Academic Community.   The academic community has not been involved with many present information management efforts and with detrimental results. Theory is not advancing, research is not being conducted in the volume that is needed, and journal articles are not keeping pace with developments in the field. As a result, students are not being exposed to information management concepts and ideas. The end result, once these students become professional practitioners, is the resistance described earlier. Academia also contains a valuable source of inexpensive research potential (theses and dissertations) that are not presently being used to develop and research information management applications.

Training Existing Personnel. Training of existing human service personnel is needed. At present, little training for human service personnel on the potentials of computerized information management exists. National training packages could be developed and contracted out to universities, national, state or local professional associations, or other training organizations. This is beginning to occur, but not with the variety and frequency that is needed.

Concluding Remarks

The computer, which has substantially changed the way information is viewed and used in business and government, is rapidly beginning to have the same impact on human services. A look at the future reveals that developments in information management are continuing at a rapid pace. Most human service professionals are not prepared to cope with these developments. Much needs to be done individually and professionally if the human services are to come to grips with the capabilities made available to them by the computer. As with other tools, we must learn to understand computers and their accompanying applications, control them, humanize them, and harness them to meet our needs.

Chapter 13

A CAUTIONARY VIEWPOINT

The potentials of the information revolution strike fear in the minds of a few people in the information management field, and rightly so. George Orwell presented us with a vision of an information management society gone mad and ugly. His novel *1984*, written in 1949, contained 137 specific predictions in the area of science, technology, and social and political life. According to Goodman (1978, p. 351), by 1972 about 80 of these predictions were in existence. In 1978, over 100 predictions had come true, and today all Orwell's predictions are technologically feasible. It seems that although George Orwell's *1984* has failed as a warning, it has succeeded brilliantly as a forecast. All the potentials for *1984* are present today.

Most forecasts of information technology are written in positive rather than negative terms. For example, we have seen forecasts of the computer's ability to contain all the information in the Library of Congress, yet not of the same computer's ability to search and change that information in accordance with someone's wishes. Yet this changing of history has happened according to Weizenbaum (1976).

> When the American president decided to bomb Cambodia and
> to keep that decision secret from the American Congress, the
> computers in the Pentagon were "fixed" to transform the
> genuine strike reports coming in from the field into the false
> reports to which government leaders were given access....
> And the high government leaders who felt themselves privi-
> leged to be allowed to read the secret reports that actually
> emerged from the Pentagon's computers of course believed
> them. After all, the computer itself had spoken. (pp. 238-239)

Bell (1979) lists three potential misuses of information
technology that should cause us concern.

1. Expansion of the techniques of surveillance.
2. Concentration of the technology of record keeping.
3. Control of access to strategic information by monopoly or
    government imposition of secrecy. (p. 32)

A fourth concern needs to be added, that is the accumulation
of the power of information by those who understand and
can afford its surrounding technology.

Probably the most potentially threatening misuse of
information technology is the keeping of records. Today a
thriving business exists in developing, merging, and selling
computerized lists of people and information about them.
When a new product, a charity, or a magazine is to be
advertised to potential customers, an organization can purchase lists of people who, by being on one list or another,
have been classified as favorably inclined to the solicitation.
The merging of numerous lists of names and accompanying
data into a flexible data base offers enormous potential for
the development of profiles of individuals who think or act
in a particular way. Recently, the CBS News documentary
"60 Minutes" had a private investigator develop a profile of
a person based on that person's computerized bank records
which, the report pointed out, are not as secure as we would
like to think. The profile was exceedingly detailed and
accurate. Lobbyists in Washington, D.C., such as the Na-

tional Rifle Association and Common Cause, are especially aware of the capacity of a computerized list. They use the computer to get their messages out to their members in key congressional districts in order to produce a flood of mail pro or con any particular piece of legislation. The National Rifle Association has been consistently successful in blocking any gun control legislation through this method even though a majority of the population favor some form of gun control. Defense lawyers with enough money can develop computerized profiles of jurists who will be sympathetic to their client's case. They then use these profiles to weed out unsympathetic prospective jurors and dramatically increase the probability of winning their case. Examples of the power and questionable use of computerized lists of people could go on and on. Our laws have not kept up with such uses of technology. Our laws have responded to abuses committed instead of providing guidance for potential new developments.

Why do we seem to be so unconcerned about the potential disastrous effects of computerized information? Certainly our history does not give us that confidence:

> The history of science and technology of the post-war era is filled with examples of reckless and unreflective "progress" which, while beneficial or at least profitable to some in the short run, may yet devastate much life on this planet. Perhaps it is too much to hope, but I hope nonetheless that as our discipline matures our practitioners will mature also, that all of us will begin to think about what we are actually doing and ponder whether, whatever it is, it is what those who follow us would want to have done. (Weizenbaum, 1978, p. 179)

Few who understand the field of computerized information management are critics of the field or are trying to help us understand what its negative potentials are. To quote Weizenbaum again,

> Today there are disagreements over programming styles, computer architecture, ways of realizing computer system security,

and so on. But, on the whole, such differences of opinion are just that—differences of opinion, not controversies. Observers from another field would, I think, be most impressed by an apparent unanimity of views in a field so large as the computer community. Where else are so many scientific and technical workers so much of one mind? (1978, p. 173)

We see extensive planning to develop, market, and make a profit off information management applications, but almost no effort in planning how to ensure that the end result is what we want for our country and for the world. Is this lack of effort due to our trust in mankind? Probably not, since we have numerous examples in history of the fact that man can be, and has been, both good and humane at times as well as evil and destructive. By examining our history we can see that the same man who is capable of love and dying for his fellow man is also capable of murdering his fellow man. The circumstances of the situation determine how man uses the potentials and the powers at his disposal, yet we seem to be doing little to ensure that the circumstances surrounding information technology provide for its being used in a positive way.

Goodman (1978) describes how little is necessary to turn the potentials of information technology into a *1984* type of reality. He uses an example of a radical band of terrorists with nuclear weapons threatening to blow up a city unless their demands are met. This potential terrorist threat triggers a mood in the country whereby measure after measure of computerized control is imposed; but since we have no plans for the imposition of technological controls in times of crisis, we have no plans for lifting these controls once the crisis is over. We need to begin the dialogue on the necessary trade-offs we as a society are willing to allow in the safety versus control issue. We need to discuss when, by whom, and how long controls can be used, and when and how they are to be dismantled; for our experience also points to an inability to eliminate a bureaucracy once it is established. Bell (1979) points out that the real threat of computerized information may not be Big Brother, but Slothful Brother.

> If anything, the real threat of such technological megalomania lies in the expansion of regulatory agencies whose rising costs and bureaucratic regulation and delays inhibit innovation and change in society. In the United States, at least, it is not Big Brother, but Slothful Brother, that becomes the problem. (p. 40)

Clearly, Bell's concern is closer to reality in the human services; for, many times, the bureaucracy becomes so fragmented and entrenched that the only integration occurring in the system is that of each individual client searching through the morass of agencies and regulations to get his or her needs met.

Another effect of information management, which should be carefully examined, is how it is structuring communications worldwide. Almost all areas of the world are affected by information technology in one form or another—for example, the radio and television.

> The computer has been incorporating itself, and will surely continue to incorporate itself, into most of the functions that are fundamental to the support, protection, and development of our society. Even now, there is no turning back, and in a few years it will be clear that we are as vitally dependent upon the information processing of our computers as upon the growth of grain in the field and the flow of fuel from the well. (Weizenbaum, 1976, p. 242)

The computer seems destined to become the underlying communications tool. Fundamental to the computer, however, is a view of the world that spreads along with it. This view of the world is what Talcott Parsons refers to as a "gloss," or a system of perception and language. Carlos Castaneda, whose novels on Don Juan, the Yaqui sorcerer, present us with a gloss totally different from our own, explains the concept of a gloss.

> A child reconnoiters the world with few preconceptions until he is taught to see things in a way that corresponds to the description everybody agrees on. The world is an agreement . . . the trick of socialization is to convince us that the description we agree upon defines the limits of the real world . . . . The system of glossing seems to be somewhat like walking. We have to learn to walk, but once we learn there is only one way to walk. We have to learn to see and talk, but once we learn we are subject to the syntax of language and the mode of perception it contains. (Keen, 1972, p. 95)

Each gloss has its advantages and disadvantages. For example, the gloss that allows the firewalker to walk through red hot coals unharmed serves no purpose for this person if he becomes stranded in New York City. Vice versa, the gloss that a Western man has which associates fire with burning will prevent him from being able to walk across hot coals. There are times when our gloss no longer helps us interpret our world, but suffocates and destroys us physically and mentally. For example, Ornstein (1972) points to the dangers of limiting man to living in only a rational, verbal, linear, causal, and logical gloss, basically the world view the computer is built on. The question becomes whether it is problematic that our world communication system is being built on a machine that is grounded in a gloss derived primarily from our Western world. How can we preserve other glosses that may be extremely useful in future activities or in making decisions, especially the more unstructured decisions?

If we examine our history, we can see how information technologies have already had a profound impact on man's capabilities. Before the printing press, whole books were memorized and recited, even by children. Today, most adults would consider such memorization tasks impossible. Similarly, we are losing our ability to perform mathematical manipulations mentally due to the use of adding machines and calculators. What capabilities will future information technologies eliminate and with what consequences?

It is essential to develop the ability to examine critically information management applications before they are developed and disseminated. Weizenbaum (1976, pp. 269-270) has taken a step in this direction by listing two types of computer applications that ought not be developed. The first are those applications that substitute a computer system for a human function that involves interpersonal respect, understanding, and love—for example, coupling the brain or visual system to a computer or installing the computer as a psychotherapist. The second type of applications to be avoided are those which do not meet a pressing need that cannot be met in any other way, and which can easily be seen to have irreversible and not entirely foreseeable side effects—for example, automated recognition of human speech. Whether one agrees with Weizenbaum or not, his efforts to open up dialogue on computer applications are a step in the right direction.

More specific to the human services, three negative impacts need closer examination.

1. The accumulation and misuse of power.
2. The protection of privacy.
3. The computer's role in providing services.

Well-managed information is powerful, and therefore information management adds power to the information it collects and stores and to the people controlling and using this information.

The negative use of power involves both means, or process, and ends. Power in the human services is negatively used if the process is not humane or the ends do not result in improved services to clients. An example of the misuse of the information management process is where a computerized budget system is used as an excuse to pay employees several weeks after the end of the month, thus allowing the agency to collect interest on a substantial amount of payroll money each year. An example of the misuse of the ends of information management is where a costly system is scrapped because it begins to document management's inefficiencies in providing services.

Computerized information highlights the typical power conflicts within an organization and throws off the balance of power that existed previous to its introduction. It offers the potential for those who gain power to take advantage of those who lose. For example, one of the continual power conflicts in agencies is whether management or the worker knows the best way to meet the needs of the client. Different information management applications shift power in this controversy in different directions. An accounting and budgeting system shifts the power in the direction of management; a computerized diagnostic tool shifts the power in the direction of the worker. In any case, the impact of this power shift should be considered before the application is developed. It may be necessary to take steps to balance out the power within the agency to keep such controversies in the realm of a healthy disagreement.

At the community level, a community data base may also change the power balance. A community data base may point out that one agency, although doing an excellent job, is optimizing one subsystem at the expense of the total system. A hospital may be providing excellent services and thus be able to grow by attracting increased funds. Yet systemwide data may show that if additional money is to be spent to save lives (a valid goal for a community health system), it must be spent in preventive care or for emergency medical services. For example, which will save more lives, a second open-heart surgery unit in the community, or education and training progams for heart-attack prevention, or the installation of trained ambulance paramedics? Similarly, a state mental hospital may be providing excellent services but preventing the development of deinstitutionalization alternatives such as group-living homes, because it means a loss of funds and power for the state hospital. The point is that we must consider how the agencies within the community will handle the power redistribution that is associated with a community data base. Mechanisms must be established to plan for the orderly handling of these potential power shifts.

The second area of negative concern about information management is the problem of privacy. Computerized client data are destructive if they fall into the wrong hands. An unsecured tape of client records can easily be removed from the agency overnight, copied, and returned with no traces that the data have been stolen. Such a tape could be a destructive force in the hands of a blackmailer or a client's potential political opponents. We have yet to eliminate the stigma of some human services as Senator Thomas Eagleton found out in his quick tenure as George McGovern's vice-presidential running mate in the 1972 presidential campaign. Mental illness still represents a "skeleton in the closet." Violations of privacy occur, not only with the release of unauthorized information outside the bureaucracy, but inside as well. Everyone probably has their own horror story, such as state civil service checking the mental health computer before hiring any civil service job applicant. Although many personnel are usually aware of privacy violations, there is usually no sense of responsibility among employees to report them, especially those that are questionable practices rather than clear-cut violations. One major reason is that channels for reporting the suspected violation without risk usually do not exist. Experience with "whistle blowing" has taught many employees that it is best to go along and not rock the boat unless they are in some sense responsible. This attitude must not be carried over into the area of client privacy.

Given the retrieval capabilities and proliferation of computerized data bases, the questions surrounding the collection, maintenance, transmission, and reporting of information the client furnishes takes on new dimensions. To what extent do clients have the right to know into what data bases the information they provide will be stored and how it will potentially be used? Should they or their legal guardian, in the case of the mentally incompetent, be informed prior to providing the information? Is written consent needed? What access should clients have to their files? Should they be allowed to delete unwanted information? This is another area where it seems the courts will be the final answer, but the courts only react after the fact and usually in cases where abuses have been alleged. What is needed is a discussion of the issues to develop guidelines to prevent abuses.

The third area, the computer's role in providing services, has been touched on by Weizenbaum in his list of applications that should not be developed. The question becomes who is responsible for deciding if the benefits of an application are more meaningful than its negative effects. Is it the developer, the funding source, the agency board, or the general public? At present it seems that responsibility falls nowhere. Should information processing chips be implanted in the brain? Who decides, the patient, the doctor, the government? Our previous experience with new therapeutic aids, such as LSD, should cause us great concern; for, in the lawsuits that followed some very questionable experimental uses of LSD, no one seems willing to take the responsibility. What shows our total lack of concern and foresight is that we have no forum on which the debate over these issues can occur.

The thrust of this book has been the potential that well-managed information offers for improving decision making and services to clients. The flaw in the equation of well-managed information equals better decisions equals improved services is the human element. If we accept the fact that humans are potentially good and bad, we should take the next step to insure that the bad does not occur. This can be done in several ways:

1. By keeping communication channels and access to information open and eliminating the jargon and mystery that surrounds sophisticated information management applications.

2. By ensuring that those who are in a position and who have the power to control are responsible to those who are potentially the controlled—for example, putting clients, consumers, client advocates, or critics on boards on advisory committees.
3. By establishing forums for discussing the potential misuses of any information management application.
4. By establishing and publicizing the clear lines of responsibility and authority for guarding against the negative effects of information management and ensuring that everyone realizes that they personally have a responsibility for guarding against negative effects, and that those who report concerns do not risk their jobs.

The destructive potential of information technology must be identified, analyzed, and minimized. The trade-offs must be brought out into the open and debated; for information technology is only as good as the people it serves.

In conclusion, this chapter has taken a negative view of information management. Those developing and applying information management technology must take this negative view seriously, for we must not let the power of computerized information parallel our disastrous and narrow-sighted handling of other technologies such as atomic power. As the nuclear arms race of today indicates, it is difficult to turn back powerful technologies once disseminated. The time to consider the negatives is before an application is developed, and the responsibility must be officially assigned within the bureaucracy even though it eventually rests with no one but ourselves.

NOTES

1. Bergwall, D. F., & Hadley, S. A. *An investigation of modeling for health planning* (U.S. Department of Health, Health Resources Administration, Education and Welfare, Bureau of Health Planning and Resource Development). Washington, D.C.: George Washington University, August 1975.

2. Boyd, K. N., & Silver, E. S. *Factors affecting the development and implementation of information systems for social services* (U.S. Department of Health, Education and Welfare, Social and Rehabilitative Service). Washington, D.C.: U.S. Department of Health, Education, and Welfare, May 1975.

3. Community Health Automated Record and Treatment System (CHARTS). Waco, Texas: Heart of Texas Region Mental Health Mental Retardation Center, 1979.

4. *CWIS, what it is, what it does.* Child Welfare Information Services, 200 Madison Ave., New York, N.Y. 10016, 1978 (photocopied).

5. Elwood, D. Clinical Psychologist, Quinco Consulting Center, Columbus, Indiana. Interview, August 15, 1977.

6. Franklin, J. L. *Management information systems in mental health.* Austin, Texas: Department of Mental Health and Mental Retardation, 1976 (photocopied).

7. Greenberg, D. Acting Director, Program Systems Division, Office of Program Systems Development, Office of Human Development, U.S. Department of Health, Education, and Welfare, Washington, D.C. Telephone interview, December 28, 1977.

8. Gunzburg, H. C. *PAC manual.* 240 Holiday St., Birmingham, England: SEFA Publication, 1973.

9. Hedlund, J. L., Vieweg, B. W., Cho, D. W., Evenson, R. C., Hickman, C. V., Holland, R. A., Vogt, S. A., Wolf, C. P., & Wood, J. B. *Mental health information systems: A state-of-the-arts report.* Columbia, Mo.: University of Missouri Health Services Research Center, June 1979 (photocopied).

10. McCurdy, B., Director, Division of Information and Services, Family Services Association of America, New York. Telephone interview, November 7, 1977.

11. Mott-McDonald Associates, Inc. *A taxonomy of Title XX social services.* Washington, D.C.: U.S. Department of Health, Education, and Welfare, Social and Rehabilitation Service, Public Services Administration, October 1975.

12. Nakamoto, R., Acting Assistant Director, Office of Information Systems, Medicaid Bureau, U.S. Department of Health, Education, and Welfare, Washington, D.C., Interview, August 5, 1977.

13. National Science Foundation. *Appropriate technology in the United States, an exploratory study.* Washington, D.C.: National Science Foundation, Exploratory Research and Systems Analysis, 1977.

14. Neilson, B. Information Systems Analyst, Office of Program Systems Development, Office of Human Development, U.S. Department of Health, Education, and Welfare, Washington, D.C. Telephone interview, October 1977.

15. Paton, J. A. President, CMHC Systems, Columbus, Ohio. Interview, December 21, 1977.

16. Racine, D. Administrative Assistant, American Public Welfare Association, Washington, D.C. Telephone interview, August 4, 1977.

17. Schnibbe, H. & Praschil, R. *State mental health statistical management information systems.* Washington, D.C.: National Association of State Mental Health Program Directors, November, 1978.

18. Schwartz, M. D. A device integrating computer assisted and videotape instruction. *Computers in Psychiatry/Psychology,* 1978, *1*(3), 10. (A bimonthly newsletter available from 26 Trumbull St., New Haven, CT.)

19. Seebohm, T. D. *Reorganization of British personal services.* Proceedings of the 125th Anniversary of the Community Service Society of New York, 1975.

20. Shute, D., Director, Office of Program Systems Development, Office of Human Development Services, U.S. Department of Health, Education, and Welfare, Washington, D.C. Telephone interview, December 22, 1978.

21. Smith, T. S., & Sorensen, J. E. (Eds.), *Integrated management information systems for community mental health centers* (U.S. Department of Health, Education, and Welfare, National Institute of Mental Health). Washington, D.C.: U.S. Department of Health, Education, and Welfare, 1974.

22. Sorensen, J. E., & Ertel, P. Peer review information systems. In I. Davidoff, M. Guttentag, & J. Offutt (Eds.), *Evaluating community mental health services: Principles and practice.* (DHEW, NIMH, Publication No. ADM 77-465) Washington, D.C., 1977.

23. Teal, F. Chief, Management Information Systems Branch, Division of Administration, Office of Human Development Services, U.S. Department of Health, Education, and Welfare, Washington, D.C. Telephone interview, January 4, 1978.

24. United Way of America. *Directory—Data processing activity.* Report of the Data Processing Service Committee. Alexandria, Va.: June 1977.

25. University of Texas at Arlington, Institute of Urban Studies. Computers and Small Local Governments Workshop, Arlington, Texas, February 23-25, 1977.

26. Yankey, J. A., and Associates. *A personal social service system for Cuyahoga county: A feasibility study.* Cleveland, Ohio: Board of Cuyahoga County Commissioners, June 30, 1977 (mimeograph).

REFERENCES

Ackoff, R. L. Management misinformation systems. *Management Science*, 1967, *14*(4), B147-B156.

Adam, R. G. Selecting and using the data dictionary. *ICP Interface*, 1978, *3*(4), 6-10.

Alexander, G. Terminal therapy. *Psychology Today*, 1978, *12*(4), 50-60.

Alter, S., & Ginzberg, M. Managing uncertainty in MIS implementation. *Sloan Management Review*, 1978, *20*, 23-31.

Amdahl, L. The technology swirl. *Datamation*, 1978, *24*(12), 18-20.

American Medical Association, Confidentiality of computerized patient information. *Computers and Medicine*, 1979, (special Report).

American Public Welfare Association, Committee on Social Services. Policy statement on personal social services. *Public Welfare*, (Special) 1977, *35*(2), 32-36.

Appleton, D. S. Manufacturing systems cookbook, part 1. *Datamation*, 1979, 26(5), 179-184. (a)

Appleton, D. S. Manufacturing systems cookbook, part 3. *Datamation*, 1979, 26(9), 130-136. (b)

Appleton, D. S. What data base isn't. *Datamation*, 1977, *23*(1), 85-92.

Bailine, S., Katzoff, A., & Rau, J. Diagnosis of schizophrenia by computer and clinicians: A pilot study. *Comprehensive Psychiatry*, 1977, *18*, 141-145.

Baker, F. The living human service organization: Application of general systems theory and research. In W. Demone, Jr. & D. Harshbarger (Eds.), *A handbook of human service organizations*, New York: Behavioral Publications, 1974.

Baldridge, J. V., & Burnham, R. A. Organizational innovation: Individual, organizational, and environmental impacts. *Administration Science Quarterly*, 1975, *20*(2), 165-175.

Barnett, A. Securing user involvement. *Data Management*, 1978, *16*, 52-57.

Becker, M. N. Sociometric location and innovativeness: Reformulation and extension of the diffusion model. *American Sociological Review*, 1970, *35*(2), 267-281.

Becker, S. W., & Whisler, T. L. The innovative organization: A selective view of current theory and research. *Journal of Business*, 1967, *40*, 462-469.

Bell, D. Thinking ahead. *Harvard Business Review*, 1979, *57*(3), 20-42.

Beltrami, E. J. *Models for public systems analysis*. New York: Academic Press, 1977.

Bertalanffy, L. V. *General system theory: Foundations, development, applications*. New York: Braziller, 1968.

Bertram, B. Defining data base administration. *ICP Interface*, 1978, *3*(4), 21-24.

Boulding, K. E. General systems theory—The skeleton of science. *Management Science*, 1956, *2*, 197-208.

Bowers, G. E., & Bowers, M. R. *The elusive unit of service*. (Project Share Human Services Monograph Series No. 1.) Washington, D.C.: U.S. Department of Health, Education, and Welfare, Office of Intergovernmental Systems, September, 1976.

Bowers, G. E. & Bowers, M. R. *Cultivating client information systems*, (Project Share Human Services Monograph Series No. 5.) Washington, D.C.: U.S. Department of Health, Education, and Welfare, Office of Intergovernmental Systems, June, 1977.

Boyd, L. H., Jr., Hylton, J. H. , & Price, S. V. Computers in social work practice: A review. *Social Work*, 1978, *23*, 368-371.

Burack, E., & Sorensen, P. F., Jr. Management preparation for computer automation: Emergent patterns and problems. *Academy of Management Journal*, 1976, *19*, 318-323.

Burch, J. G., Jr., Strater, F. R., & Grudnitski, G. *Information systems: Theory and practice* (2nd ed.). New York: Wiley, 1979.

Byrd, J., Jr. *Operations research models for public administration*. Lexington, Mass.: Heath, 1975.

Carlisle, H. M. *Management: Concepts and situations*. Chicago: Science Research Associates, 1976.

Carlson, E. D. Decision support systems: Personal computing services for managers. *Management Review*, 1977, *66*, 4-11.

Carper, W. B. Human factors in MIS. *Journal of Systems Management*, 1977, *28*(11), 48-50.

Carter, D. E. & Newman, F. L. A client-oriented system of mental health service delivery and program management: A workbook and guide. (NIMH Series C, No. 12, DHEW publication No. ADM 76-307.) Washington, D.C.: U.S. Government Printing Office, 1976.

Cassell, R. N. Computer assist counseling (CASCON). *Psychology*, 1975, *12*, 3-9.

Caswell, S. A. Computer peripherals: A revolution is coming. *Datamation*, 1979, *25*(6), 82-87.

Catastrophe theory. *Newsweek*, January 19, 1976, pp. 54-55.

Chapman, R. L. The design of management information systems for mental health organizations: A primer. (NIMH Series C, No. 13, DHEW publication No. ADM 76-333.) Washington, D.C.: U.S. Government Printing Office, 1976.

Churchman, C. W. *The systems approach*. New York: Dell, 1968.

Cobb, C. W. Problems and principles in the development of management information systems. *International Journal of Mental Health*, 1976-77, *5*(4), 103-120.

Coddington, D. R., & King, T. L. Automated history taking in child psychiatry. *American Journal of Psychiatry*, 1972, *129*(3), 52-58.

Colby, K. M. *Artificial paranoia: A computer simulation of paranoid processes*. New York: Pergamon, 1976.

Computer society. *Time*, February 20, 1978, pp. 44-59.

Cooper, M. Guidelines for a minimum statistical and accounting system for community mental health centers. (NIMH Series C, No. 7, DHEW publication No. ADM 77-14.) Washington, D.C.: U.S. Government Printing Office, 1973.

Corwin, R. G. Strategies for organizational innovation: An empirical comparison. *American Sociological Review*, 1972, *37*, 441-454.

Crawford, J. L., Morgan, D. W., & Gianturco, D. T. *Progress in mental health information systems: Computer applications*. Cambridge, Mass.: Ballinger, 1974.

Czepiel, J. A. Patterns of interorganizational communications and the diffusion of a major technological innovation in a competitive industrial community. *Academy of Management Journal*, 1975, *18*, 6-25.

Daniel, L. M. Planning MIS acceptance. *Journal of Systems Management*, 1976, *27*, 20-21.

Danziger, J. N. Computers, local governments, and the litany to EDP. *Public Administration Review*, 1977, *37*, 28-37.

Davis, D., & Allen, R. The evolution of a management information system in an outpatient mental health institute. *Administration in Mental Health*, 1979, *6*, 225-239.

Davis, G. B. *Management information systems: Conceptual foundations, structure, and development*. New York: McGraw-Hill, 1974.

Davis, R. M. Evolution of computers and computing. *Science*, 1977, *195*(4283), 1096-1102.

Deen, S. M. *Fundamentals of data base systems.* New York: Hayden, 1977.

DeMoll, L. (Ed.). *Rainbook: Resources for appropriate technology.* New York: Schocken Books, 1977.

DeWitt, J. *Managing the human service "system": What have we learned from service integration?* (Project Share Human Service Monograph Series No. 4.) Washington, D.C.: Department of HEW, Office of Intergovernmental Systems, August, 1977.

Dial, O. E., & Goldberg, E. M. *Privacy, security, and computers—Guidelines for municipal and other public information systems.* New York: Praeger, 1975.

Dickson, J. W. The adoption of innovative proposals as risky choice: A model and some results. *Academy of Management Journal*, 1976, *19*(2), 291-302.

Doliner, I. Word processing systems: Points to consider. *Creative Computing*, 1979, *5*(5), 28-30.

Downs, A. A realistic look at the final payoffs from urban data systems. *Public Administration Review*, 1967, 27, 204-210.

Dreyer, L., Bellerby, L., & Koroloff, N. *MIS perspectives.* Portland, Oregon: Curriculum Development MIS Project, Regional Research Institute for Human Services, Portland State University, 1979.

Drummond, H. Pocketa pocketa machines. *Mother Jones*, 1978, *3*, 9-10.

Dutton, W. H., & Kraemer, K. L. The automation of bias: Computers and local government budgeting. Irvine, CA: Public Policy Research Organization, University of California, Irvine.

Ein-Dor, P., & Segev, E. *Managing management information systems.* Lexington, Mass.: Heath, 1978. (a)

Ein-Dor, P., & Segev, E. Organizational context and the success of management information systems. *Management Science*, 1978, *24*, 1064-1077. (b)

Ein-Dor, P., & Segev, E. Strategic planning for management information systems. *Management Science*, 1978, *24*, 1631-1641. (c)

Exley, C. E., Jr. "Friendly" computers will cut computer labor costs. *The Futurist*, 1977, *11*, 396.

Fein, E. A data system for an agency. *Social Work*, 1975, *20*, 21-24.

Flagle, C. D., Huggins, W. H., & Roy, R. H. (Eds.). *Operations research and systems engineering.* Baltimore: Johns Hopkins Press, 1960.

Fried, L. MIS success story: Smoothing out people system. *Data Management*, 1977, *15*(7), 30-36.

Gall, J. *Systemantics: How systems work and especially how they fail.* New York: Pocket Books, 1975.

Gass, S. I., & Sisson, R. L. *A guide to models in government planning and operations*. Potomac, Md.: Sauger Books, 1975.

George, C. S., Jr. *The History of Management Thought* (2nd ed.) Englewood Cliffs: Prentice-Hall, 1972.

Getting control of the system. *Dun's Review*, 1977, *110*, 66-81.

Getz, C. W. DP's role is changing. *Datamation*, 1978, *24*(2), 117-128.

Gibson, C. F., & Nolan, R. L. Managing the four stages of EDP growth. *Harvard Business Review*, 1974, *52*, 76-88.

Gilbert, J. C. Can today's MIS manager make the transition? *Datamation*, 1978, *24*(3), 141-151.

Goodman, D. Countdown to 1984: Big Brother may be right on schedule. *The Futurist*, 1978, *12*, 345-355.

Gorry, G. A., & Morton, M. S. A framework for management information systems. *Sloan Management Review*, 1971, *13*, 55-70.

Gray, V. Innovation in the states: A diffusion study. *The American Political Science Review*, 1973, *67*(4), 1174-85.

Gregory, N. Congress—The politics of information. *Data Management*, 1978, *16*, 96-100.

Hagebak, B. R. Local human service delivery: The integration imperative. *Public Administration Review*, 1979, *36*, 575-582.

Hanold, T. An executive view of MIS. *Datamation*, 1972, *18*(11), 65-71.

Harvard Law Review. Mental health litigation: Implementing institutional reform. *Mental Disability Law Reporter*, 1977, *2*, 221-233.

Hasenfeld, Y. People processing organizations: An exchange approach. *American Sociological Review*, 1972, *37*, 256-63.

Havelock, R. G., Guskin, A., Frohman, M., Havelock, M., Hill, M., & Huber, J. *Planning for innovation*. Ann Arbor, Mich.: Center for Research on Utilization of Scientific Knowledge, 1969.

Heintz, K. G. State organizations for human services. *Evaluation*, 1976, *3*, 106-110.

Herriott, R. E., & Hodgkins, B. J. Social context and the school: An open systems analysis of school and educational change. In Y. Hasenfeld & R. A. English (Eds.), *Human Service Organizations*. Ann Arbor, Mich.: University of Michigan Press, 1974.

Herzlinger, R. Why data systems in nonprofit organizations fail. *Harvard Business Review*, 1977, *55*, 81-86.

Hobbs, L. C. A look at the future. *Computer*, 1976, *9*, 9-10.

Horton, W., Jr., Budgeting the data and information resource. *Journal of Systems Management*, 1977, *28*(2), 12-14. (a)

Horton, W. W., Jr. Information resources management: Fad or fact? *Journal of Systems Management*, 1977, *28*(12), 6-9. (b)

Hoshino, G., & McDonald, T. P. Agencies in the computer age. *Social Work*, 1975, *20*, 10-14.

Joseph, E. C. Future smart systems. *Data Management*, 1978, *16*, 72-80.

Kahn, A. J., & Kamerman, S. B. *Social services in international perspective.* Washington, D.C.: U.S. Government Printing Office, 1976.

Kahne, S., Lefkowitz, I., & Rose, C. Automatic control by distributed intelligence. *Scientific American*, 1979, *240*(6), 78-90.

Katz, D., & Kahn, R. L. Common characteristics of open systems. In F. E. Emery (Ed.), *Systems thinking.* Middlesex, England: Penguin Books, 1969.

Keen, P. G., & Morton, M. S. *Decision support systems: An organizational perspective.* Reading, Mass.: Addison-Wesley, 1978.

Keen, S. Sorcerer's apprentice, a conversation with Carlos Castaneda. *Psychology Today*, 1972, *6*(7), 90-102.

Kirkley, J. L. Editor's readout. *Datamation*, 1979, *25*, 7.

Klein, M. H., Greist, J. H., & Van Cura, L. J. Computers in psychiatry. *Archives of General Psychiatry*, 1975, *32*, 837-843.

Kleinschrod, W. A. *Management's guide to word processing.* Chicago: Dartnell Corporation, 1977.

Kluess, P. W., & Moyer, M. G. COMPIS, GBF/DIME, and human resources: A local application. *Proceedings of the 16th Annual Conference of the Urban and Regional Information Systems Association*, August, 1978, pp. 268-278.

Knight, K. E. A descriptive model of the intra-firm innovation process. *Journal of Business*, 1967, *40*(4), 478-496.

Kraemer, K. L. Local government, information systems, and technology transfer: Evaluating some common assertions about computer application transfer. *Public Administration Review*, 1977, *37*, 368-382.

Kraemer, K. L., & King, J. L. *Computers, power, and urban management: What every local executive should know.* Sage Professional Papers in Administration and Policy Studies, Series no. 03-031, Beverly Hills, Calif.: Sage Publications, 1976.

Laska, E. M., & Bank, R. (Eds.). *Safeguarding psychiatric privacy: Computer systems and their uses.* New York: Wiley, 1975.

Lawler, E. E. Adaptive experiments: An approach to organizational behavior research. *Academy of Management Review*, 1977, *2*, 576-585.

Lefkovits, H. C. *Data dictionary systems.* Wellesley, Mass.: QED Information Sciences, 1977.

Lin, N., & Burt, R. S. Differential effects of information channels in the process of innovation diffusion. *Social Forces*, 1975, *54*, 256-270.

Lopez-Toledo, A. A. A controlled Markov chain model for nursing homes. *Simulation*, 1976, *27*(5), 161-169.

Lucas, H. C., Jr. *Information systems concepts for management.* New York: McGraw-Hill, 1978.

Lucas, H. C., Jr. Performance and the use of an information system. *Management Science*, 1975, *21*, 908-919.

Lucas, R. W. A study of patients' attitudes to computer interrogation. *International Journal of Man-Machine Studies*, 1977, *9*, 69-86.

Lynn, L. E., Jr., & Seidl, J. M. The mega-proposal. *Evaluation*, 1976, *3*, 111-114.

Lyon, J. K. *The database administrator.* New York: Wiley, 1976.

March, J. G., & Simon, H. A. *Organizations.* New York: Wiley, 1958.

Maronde, R. F. Computer monitoring of psychotropic drug prescriptions. *Journal of Continuing Education in Psychiatry*, 1978, *39*, 11.

Martino, J. P. Telecommunications in the year 2000. *The Futurist*, 1979, *13*, 95-104.

Mason, R. O., & Mitroff, I. I. A program for research on management information systems. *Management Science*, 1973, *19*, 475-485.

Matthews, D. Q. *The design of the management information system* (Rev. ed.). New York: Petrocelli/Charter, 1976.

Maypole, D. E. Developing a management information system in a rural community mental health center. *Administration in Mental health*, 1978, *6*, 69-80.

McCracken, D. D. The changing face of applications programming. *Datamation*, 1978, *24*(12), 24-30.

McRobie, G. Why the world will shift to intermediate technology. *The Futurist*, 1977, *11*, 83-89.

Meldman, M. J., Harris, D., Pellicore, R. J., & Johnson, E. I. A computer-assisted, goal-oriented psychiatric progress note system. *American Journal of Psychiatry*, 1977, *134*, 38-40.

Milio, N. Health care organizations and innovation. *Journal of Health and Social Behavior*, 1971, *12*(2), 163-173.

Miller, J. G. The nature of living systems. *Behavioral Science*, 1976, *21*(2), 296-320.

Minami, W. N. Data administration. *Journal of Systems Management*, 1976, *27*(5), 40-44.

Mintzberg, H. Reviews of the new science of management decision, revised edition. *Administrative Science Quarterly*, 1977, *22*, 342-50.

Mittenthal, S. D. A system approach to human services integration. *Evaluation*, 1976, *3*, 142-148.

Murdick, R. G., & Ross, J. E. *Information systems for modern management* (2nd ed.). Englewood Cliffs, N.J.: Prentice-Hall, 1975.

National health planning and resource development act of 1974 (Public Law 93-641). Washington, D.C.: U.S. Congress, January 4, 1975.

Neu, C. W. Small EDP shop risks. *Journal of Systems Management*, 1976, *27*(6), 36-39.

Newman, W. H. *Constructive control: Design and use of control systems.* Englewood Cliffs, N.J.: Prentice-Hall, 1975.

Newsweek, May 14, 1979, p. 29.

Noah, J. C. Information systems in human services: Misconceptions, deceptions, and ethics. *Administration in Mental Health*, 1978, *5*(2), 99-111.

Nolan, R. L. Managing the crises in data processing. *Harvard Business Review*, 1979, *57*(2), 115-126.

Noyce, R. N. Large-scale integration: What is yet to come? *Science*, 1977, *195*(4283), 1102-1106.

Ornstein, R. E. *The psychology of consciousness*. San Francisco: Freeman, 1972.

Paton, J. A., & D'Huyvetter, P. K. *Management information systems for mental health agencies: A planning and acquisition guide*. (NIMH Statistical Report.) Washington, D.C.: U.S. Department of Health, Education, and Welfare, National Institute of Mental Health, 1980 (in press).

Patterson, P. A. Recent developments in urban gaming. *Simulation*, 1976, *26*(2), 62-64.

Patti, R. J. Patterns of management activity in social welfare agencies. *Administration in Social Work*, 1977, *1*, 5-18.

Percy, E. A. Incremental improvement of a community mental health center management information system. *Evaluation*, 1977, *4*, 205-207.

Phillippakis, A. S., & Kazmier, L. J. *Structured* COBOL. New York: McGraw-Hill, 1977.

Piecewicz, R. E. Computers and society: Some principles, theorems, and assertions. *Computers and People*, 1977, *26*(4), 13-16.

Pierce, J. R. *Symbols, signals, and noise: The nature and process of communication*. New York: Harper & Row, 1961.

Polivy, D., & Salvatore, T. Constraints on effective information system development and use in the voluntary human service sector. *Proceedings from the 14th Annual Conference of the Urban and Regional Information Systems Association*, Atlanta, Georgia, September, 1976, pp. 57-68.

Quinn, R. E. The impact of a computerized information system on the integration and coordination of human services. *Public Administration Review*, 1976, *36*(2), 166-174.

Redburn, F. S. On "human services integration." *Public Administration Review*, 1977, *37*, 264-269.

Reich, T., Robins, L. N., Woodruff, R. A., Tailbleson, M., Rich, C., & Cunningham, L. Computer-assisted derivation of a screening interview for alcoholism. *Archives of General Psychiatry*, 1975, *32*, 847-852.

Report of the Commission on Federal Paperwork (Final summary report). Washington, D.C.: U.S. Government Printing Office, 1977.

Rittersbach, G. H. Modes of EDP for the small business. *Management Controls*, 1975, *22*, 108-114.

Robinson, J. O. The computer in clinical psychology. In J. Apter & G. Westby (Eds.), *The computer in psychology.* New York: Wiley, 1973.

Rogers, E. M. *Diffusion in innovations.* New York: Free Press, 1962.

Rogers, E. M., & Shoemaker, F. F. *Communication of innovations.* New York: Free Press, 1971.

Roland, J. The microelectronic revolution. *The Futurist,* 1979, *13,* 81-90.

Roles for general purpose governments in service integration. (Project Share Human Service Monograph, Series No. 2.) Washington, D.C.: U.S. Department of Health, Education, and Welfare, Office of Intergovernmental Systems, August, 1976.

Rose, J., (Ed.). *Survey of cybernetics.* New York: Gordon and Breach Science Publishers, 1969.

Rosie, A. M. Cybernetics and information (Information theory problems). in J. Rose (Ed.), *Survey of cybernetics.* New York: Gordon and Breach Science Publishers, 1969.

Ross, J. E. *Modern management and information systems.* Reston, Va.: Reston Publishing, 1976.

Rothman, J., Erlich, J. L., & Teresa, J. G. *Promoting innovation and change in organizations and communities: A planning manual.* New York: Wiley, 1976.

Rowe, L. A., & Boise, W. B. Organizational innovation: Current research and evolving concepts. *Public Administration Review,* 1974, *34*(3), 284-293.

Rubinstein, M. F. *Patterns of problem solving.* Englewood Cliffs, N.J.: Prentice-Hall, 1975.

Sapolsky, H. M. Organizational structure and innovation. *Journal of Business,* 1967, *40*(4), 497-510.

Sashkin, M., Morris, W. C., & Horst, L. A comparison of social and organizational change models: Information flow and data use processes. *Psychological Review,* 1973, *80*(6), 510-526.

Schewe, C. D. The management information system user: An exploratory behavioral analysis. *Academy of Management Journal,* 1976, *19*(4), 577-590.

Schoderbek, P., Kefalas, A., & Schoderbek, C. *Management systems: Conceptual considerations.* Dallas: Business Publications, 1975.

Schoech, D., & Arangio, T. Computers in the human services. *Social Work,* 1979, *24,* 96-102.

Schoech, D. J. & Schkade, L. L. Planning for the coming growth of computerized data processing in human services. *Public Welfare,* 1980, 38 (in press).

Schulberg, H. C., & Baker, F. (Eds.), *Developments in human services.* (Vol. II) New York: Behavioral Publications, 1975.

Schumacher, E. F. *Small is beautiful.* New York: Harper & Row, 1973.

Semprevivo, P. C. *Systems analysis: Definition, process, and design.* Chicago: Science Research Associates, 1976.

Shepard, H. A. Innovation-resisting and innovation-producing organizations. *Journal of Business,* 1967, *40*(4), 470-477.

Shuman, E. Computerized psychiatric diagnostic tests. *Human Behavior,* 1976, *5*(8), 56-59.

Simmons, W. W. The concensor: A new tool for decision-makers. *The Futurist,* 1979, *13*(2), 91-95.

Simon, H. A. *Administrative behavior* (3rd ed.). New York: Free Press, 1945.

Simon, H. A. *The new science of management decision.* New York: Harper & Row, 1960.

Simon, H. A. *The new science of management decision* (Rev. ed.). Englewood Cliffs, N. J.: Prentice-Hall, 1977. (a)

Simon, H. A. What computers mean for man and society. *Science,* 1977, *195*(4283), 1186-1191. (b)

Singh, J. *Great ideas in information theory language and cybernetics.* New York: Dover, 1966.

Slack, W. V., & Slack, C. W. Talking to a computer about emotional problems: A comparative study. *Psychotherapy: Theory, Research and Practice,* 1977, *14*, 156-164.

Slavin, S. (Ed.) *Social administration: The management of the social services.* New York: Haworth Press, 1978.

Software industry by 1984: "Big Brother's a nice guy." *Data Management,* 1977, *15*, 12-13.

Spangle, C. W. Impact of distributed systems. *Data Management,* 1978, *16*, 15-18.

Spitzer, R. L., & Endicott, J. Can the computer assist clinicians in psychiatric diagnosis? *American Journal of Psychiatry,* 1974, *131*, 523-30.

Stein, I. *Systems theory, science, and social work.* Englewood Cliffs, N.J.: Scarecrow Press, 1974.

Stewart, R. *How computers affect management.* Cambridge, Mass.: M.I.T. Press, 1971.

Stone, L. A., & Kristjanson, R. W. Computer-assisted group encounter. *Small Group Behavior,* 1975, *6*(4), 457-468.

Sustaining worthwhile innovations in mental health organizations. *Evaluation,* 1976, *3*, 10.

Text. *Mental Disability Law Reporter,* 1977, *1*, 474-475.

Thomas, E. J., Walter, C. L., & O'Flaherty, K. Computer-assisted assessment and modification: Possibilities and illustrative data. *Social Service Review,* 1974, *48*(2), 170-182.

Toffler, A. *Future shock.* New York: Random House, 1970.

Tomeski, E. *The executive use of computers*. New York: MacMillan, 1969.

Vail, H. The automated office. *The Futurist*, 1978, *12*, 73-78.

Van Gigch, J. P. *Applied general systems theory*. New York: Harper & Row, 1974.

Vondracek, F. W., Urban, H. B., & Parsonage, W. H. Feasibility of an automated intake procedure for human service workers. *Social Service Review*, 1974, *48*(2), 271-278.

Vyssotsky, V. A., Computer systems in business: more evolution than revolution. *Management Review*, 1979, *68*, 15-16.

Weiner, M. E. *Application of organization and systems theory to human services reform*. (Project Share Human Service Monograph Series No. 6.) Washington, D.C.: U.S. Department of Health, Education, and Welfare, Office of Intergovernmental Systems, April 1978.

Weizenbaum, J. *Computer power and human reason*. San Francisco: Freeman, 1976.

Weizenbaum, J. Controversies and responsibilities. *Datamation*, 1978, *24*(12), 173-179.

Whisler, T. L. *The impact of computers on organizations*. New York: Praeger, 1970.

Wiener, N. *Cybernetics or control and communication in the animal and the machine*. New York: Wiley, 1948.

Wilder, J. F., & Miller, S. Management information. In S. Feldman (Ed.), *The administration of mental health services*. Springfield, Ill.: C. C. Thomas, 1973.

Williams, T. A. (Presider). Session VI—on line assessment and evaluation. *Behavior Research Methods and Instrumentation*, 1977, *9*(2), 108-143.

Williams, T. A., Johnson, J. H., & Bliss, E. A computer-assisted psychiatric unit. *American Journal of Psychiatry*, 1975, *132*, 1074-1076.

Wilson, J. Q. Innovation in organization: Notes toward a theory. In J. D. Thompson (Ed.), *Approaches to organizational design*. Pittsburgh: University of Pittsburgh Press, 1966, 193-219.

Wohl, A. A review of office automation. *Datamation*, 1980, 26(2), 117-119.

Wohl, A. D. Word processing 1979: A market in evolution. *Datamation*, 1979, *25*(6), 112-114.

Worthley, J. A. Computers and management: Taming the technological environment of public administration. *Public Administration Review*, 1978, *38*, 290-293.

Wuori v. *Zitnay*, No. 75-80-SD (D. Maine July 14, 1978). *Mental Disability Law Reporter*, 1978, *2*, 729-740.

Zaltman, G., Duncan, R., & Holbek, J. *Innovations and organizations*. New York: Wiley, 1973.

AUTHOR INDEX

303

SUBJECT INDEX